# CHARLES DARWIN

# CHARLES DARWIN

GRANT ALLEN,
ANDREW LANG

9 789356 146891
ISBN: 978-93-5614-689-1

Published: 1885



LECTOR HOUSE

LECTOR HOUSE LLP
E-MAIL: info@lectorhouse.com

ENGLISH WORTHIES

# CHARLES DARWIN

BY

GRANT ALLEN

EDITED BY
ANDREW LANG

1885

# PREFACE.

In this little volume I have endeavoured to present the life and work of Charles Darwin viewed as a moment in a great revolution, in due relation both to those who went before and to those who come after him. Recognising, as has been well said, that the wave makes the crest, not the crest the wave, I have tried to let my hero fall naturally into his proper place in a vast onward movement of the human intellect, of which he was himself at once a splendid product and a moving cause of the first importance. I have attempted to show him both as receiving the torch from Lamarck and Malthus, and as passing it on with renewed brilliancy to the wide school of evolutionary thinkers whom his work was instrumental in arousing to fresh and vigorous activity along a thousand separate and varied lines of thought and action.

As Mr. Francis Darwin was already engaged upon a life of his father, I should have shrunk from putting forth my own little book if I had not succeeded in securing beforehand his kind sanction. That sanction, however, was at once so frankly and cordially given, that all my hesitation upon such a score was immediately laid aside; and as I have necessarily had to deal rather with Darwin's position as a thinker and worker than with the biographical details of his private life, I trust the lesser book may not clash with the greater, but to some extent may supplement and even illustrate it.

Treating my subject mainly as a study in the interaction of organism and environment, it has been necessary for me frequently to introduce the names of living men of science side by side with some of those who have more or less recently passed away from among us. For uniformity's sake, as well as for brevity's, I have been compelled, in every instance alike, to omit the customary conventional handles. I trust those who thus find themselves docked of their usual titles of respect will kindly remember that the practice is in fact adopted *honoris causâ*; they are paying prematurely the usual penalty of intellectual greatness.

My obligations to Professor Huxley, to Professor Fiske, to Mr. Herbert Spencer, to Professor Sachs, to Hermann Müller, to Dr. Krause, to Charles Darwin himself, and to many other historians and critics of evolutionism, will be sufficiently obvious to all instructed readers, and are for the most part fully acknowledged already in the text. It would be absurd to overload so small and popularly written a book with references and authorities. I hope, therefore, that any other writers to whom I may inadvertently have neglected to confess my debts will kindly rest satisfied with this general acknowledgment. There are, however, three persons in particular from whom I have so largely borrowed facts or ideas that I owe them more special and definite thanks. From Mr. Woodall's admirable paper on Charles Darwin, contributed to the 'Transactions of the Shropshire Archæological Society,' I have taken much interesting information about my hero's immediate ancestry and early days. From Mr. Samuel Butler, the author of 'Evolution Old and New,' I have derived many pregnant suggestions with regard to the true position and meaning of Buffon, Erasmus Darwin, and the early essentially teleological evolutionists—suggestions which I am all the more anxious to acknowledge since I differ fundamentally from Mr. Butler in his estimate of the worth of Charles Darwin's distinctive discovery of natural selection. Finally, to Mr. Bates, the 'Naturalist on the Amazons,' I am indebted for several valuable items of information as to the general workings of the pre-Darwinian evolutionary spirit.

In a book dealing so largely with a contemporary movement, the history of which has never yet been consecutively written down in full, or subjected as a whole to searching criticism, there must probably be many errors of detail, which can hardly be avoided under such circumstances. I have endeavoured to minimise them as far as possible. For those which may have escaped my own scrutiny I must trust both for correction and for indulgence to the kindness of my readers.

# CONTENTS

# CHARLES DARWIN

## CHAPTER I.

## THE WORLD INTO WHICH DARWIN WAS BORN.

Charles Darwin was a great man, and he accomplished a great work. The Newton of biology, he found the science of life a chaotic maze; he left it an orderly system, with a definite plan and a recognisable meaning. Great men are not accidents; great works are not accomplished in a single day. Both are the product of adequate causes. The great man springs from an ancestry competent to produce him; he is the final flower and ultimate outcome of converging hereditary forces, that culminate at last in the full production of his splendid and exceptional personality. The great work which it is his mission to perform in the world is never wholly of his own inception. It also is the last effect of antecedent conditions, the slow result of tendencies and ideas long working unseen or but little noticed beneath the surface of opinion, yet all gradually conspiring together towards the definitive revolution at whose head, in the fulness of time, the as yet unborn genius is destined to place himself. This is especially the case with those extraordinary waves of mental upheaval, one of which gave us the Italian renaissance, and another of which is actually in progress around us at the present day. They have their sources deep down in the past of human thought and human feeling, and they are themselves but the final manifestation of innumerable energies which have long been silently agitating the souls of nations in their profoundest depths.

Thus, every great man may be regarded as possessing two distinct lines of ancestry, physical and spiritual, each of which separately demands elucidation. He owes much in one way to his father and his mother, his grandfathers and his grandmothers, and his remoter progenitors, from some or all of whom he derives, in varying degrees and combinations, the personal qualities whose special interaction constitutes his greatness and his idiosyncrasy; he owes much in another way to his intellectual and moral ancestors, the thinkers and workers who have preceded him in his own department of thought or action, and have made possible in the course of ages the final development of his special revolution or his particular system. Viewed as an individual, he is what he is, with all his powers and faculties and potentialities, in virtue of the brain, the frame, the temperament, the energy he inherits directly from his actual ancestors, paternal and maternal; viewed as a factor or element in a great movement, he is what he is because the movement had succeeded in reaching such and such a point in its progress already without him, and waited only for such and such a grand and commanding personality in order to carry it yet a step further on its course of development.

No man who ever lived would more cordially have recognised these two alternative aspects of the great worker's predetermining causes than Charles Darwin. He knew well that the individual is the direct cumulative product of his physical predecessors, and that he works and is worked upon in innumerable ways by the particular environment into whose midst he is born. Let us see, then, in his own case what were these two main sets of conditioning circumstances which finally led up to the joint production of Charles Darwin, the man and the philosopher, the thinking brain and the moving energy. In other words, what was the state of the science of life at the time when he first began to observe and to speculate; and what was the ancestry which made him be born a person capable of helping it forward at a single bound over its great restricting dogmatic barrier of the fixity of species?

Let us begin, in the first place, by clearing the path beforehand of a popular misconception, so extremely general and almost universal that, unless it be got rid of at the very outset of our sketch, much of the real scope and purport of Darwin's life and work must, of necessity, remain entirely misunderstood by the vast mass of English readers. In the public mind Darwin is, perhaps, most commonly regarded as the discoverer and founder of the evolution hypothesis. Two ideas are usually associated with his name and memory. It is believed that he was the first propounder of the theory which supposes all plant and animal forms to be the result, not of special creation, but of slow modification in pre-existent organisms. It is further and more particularly believed that he was the first propounder of the theory which supposes the descent of man to be traceable from a remote and more or less monkey-like ancestor. Now, as a matter of fact, Darwin was not the prime originator of either of these two great cardinal ideas. Though he held both as part of his organised theory of things, he was not by any means the first or the earliest thinker to hold them or to propound them publicly. Though he gained for them both a far wider and more general acceptance than they had ever before popularly received, he laid no sort of claim himself to originality or proprietorship in either theory. The grand idea which he did really originate was not the idea of 'descent with modification,' but the idea of 'natural selection,' by which agency, as he was the first to prove, definite kinds of plants and animals have been slowly evolved from simpler forms, with definite adaptations to the special circumstances by which they are surrounded. In a word, it was the peculiar glory of Charles Darwin, not to have suggested that all the variety of animal and vegetable life might have been produced by slow modifications in one or more original types, but to have shown the nature of the machinery by which such a result could be actually attained in the practical working out of natural causes. He did not invent the development theory, but he made it believable and comprehensible. He was not, as most people falsely imagine, the Moses of evolutionism, the prime mover in the biological revolution; he was the Joshua who led the world of thinkers and workers into full fruition of that promised land which earlier investigators had but dimly descried from the Pisgah-top of conjectural speculation.

How far Darwin's special idea of natural selection supplemented and rendered credible the earlier idea of descent with modification we shall see more fully when we come to treat of the inception and growth of his great epoch-making work, 'The Origin of Species;' for the present, it must suffice to point out that in the world into which he was born, the theory of evolution already existed in a more or less shadowy and undeveloped shape. And since it was his task in life to raise this theory from the rank of a mere plausible and happy guess to the rank of a highly elaborate and almost universally accepted biological system, we may pause awhile to consider on the threshold what was the actual state of natural science at the moment when the great directing and organising intelligence of Charles Darwin first appeared.

From time immemorial, in modern Christendom at least, it had been the general opinion of learned and simple alike that every species of plant or animal owed its present form and its original existence to a distinct act of special creation. This *naïf* belief, unsupported as it was by any sort of internal evidence, was supposed to rest directly upon the express authority of a few obscure statements in the Book of Genesis. The Creator, it was held, had in the beginning formed each kind after a particular pattern, had endowed it with special organs devised with supreme wisdom for subserving special functions, and had bestowed upon it the mystical power of reproducing its like in its own image to all generations. No variation of importance ever occurred within the types thus constituted; all plants and animals always retained their special forms unaltered in any way from era to era. This is the doctrine of the fixity and immutability of species, almost universal in the civilised world up to the end of the last century.

Improbable as such a crude idea now seems to any person even moderately acquainted with the extraordinary variety and variability of living forms, it nevertheless contained nothing at all likely to contradict the ordinary experience of the everyday observer in the last century. The handful of plants and animals with which he was personally acquainted consisted for the most part of a few large, highly advanced, and well-marked forms, not in the least liable to be mistaken for one another even by the most hasty and casual spectator. A horse can immediately be discriminated by the naked eye from a donkey, and a cow from a sheep, without risk of error; nobody is likely to confuse wheat with barley, or to hesitate between classing any given fruit that is laid before him as a pear or an apple, a plum or a nectarine. Variability seldom comes under the notice of the ordinary passing spectator as it does under that of the prying and curious scientific observer; and when it comes at all, as in the case of dogs and pigeons, roses and hyacinths, it is no doubt set down carelessly on a superficial view as a mere result of human selection or of deliberate mongrel interbreeding. To the eye of the average man, all the living objects ordinarily perceived in external nature fall at once under certain fixed and recognisable kinds, as dogs and horses, elms and ashes, whose limits he is never at all inclined to confound in any way one with the other.

Linnæus, the great father of modern scientific biology, had frankly and perhaps unthinkingly accepted this current and almost universal dogma of the fixity and immutability of species. Indeed, by defining a kind as a group of plants or animals so closely resembling one another as to give rise to the belief that they might all be descended from a single ancestor or pair of ancestors, he implicitly gave the new sanction of his weighty authority to the creation hypothesis, and to the prevalent doctrine of the unchangeability of organic forms. To Linnæus, the species into which he mapped out all the plants and animals then known, appeared as the descendants each of a solitary progenitor or of a primitive couple, called into existence at the beginning of all things by the direct fiat of a designing Creator. He saw the world of organic life as composed of so many well-demarcated types, each separate, distinct, and immutable, each capable of producing its like *ad infinitum*, and each unable to vary from its central standard in any of its individuals, except perhaps within very narrow and unimportant limits.

But towards the close of the eighteenth century, side by side with the general awakening of the human intellect and the arrival of a new era of free social investigation, which culminated in a fresh order of things, there was developed a more critical and sceptical attitude in the world of science, which soon produced a notable change of front among thinking naturalists as to the origin and meaning of specific distinctions.

Buffon was the first great biological innovator who ventured, in very doubtful and tentative language, to suggest the possibility of the rise of species from one another by slow modification of ancestral forms. Essentially a popular essayist, writing in the volcanic priest-suppressed France of the *ancien régime*, during the inconsistent days of Louis XV. and Louis XVI., when it was uncertain whether novel and heterodox opinions would bring down upon their author fame and reputation or the Sorbonne and the Bastille, Buffon was careful to put his conjectural conclusions in a studiously guarded and often even ironical form. But time after time, in his great discursive work, the 'Histoire Naturelle' (published in successive volumes between 1749 and 1788), he recurs anew to the pregnant suggestion that plants and animals may not be bound by fixed and immovable limits of species, but may freely vary in every direction from a common centre, so that one kind may gradually and slowly be evolved by natural causes from the type of another. He points out that, underlying all external diversities of character and shape, fundamental likenesses of type occur in many animals, which irresistibly suggest the novel notion of common descent from a single ancestor. Thus regarded, he says, not only the ass and the horse (to take a particular passage) but even man himself, the monkeys, the quadrupeds, and all vertebrate animals, might be viewed as merely forming divergent branches of one and the same great family tree. Every such family, he believed, whether animal or vegetable, might have sprung originally from a single stock, which after many generations had here developed into a higher form, and there degenerated into a lower and less perfect type of organisation. Granting this—granting that nature could by slow variation produce one species in the course of direct descent from another unlike it (for example, the ass from the horse), then, Buffon observed, there was no further limit to be set to her powers in this respect, and we might reasonably conclude that from a single primordial being she has gradually been able in the course of time to develop the whole continuous gamut of existing animal and vegetable life. To be sure, Buffon always saves himself from censure by an obvious afterthought—'But no; it is certain from revelation that every species was directly created by a separate fiat.' This half-hearted and somewhat subrisive denial, however, must be taken merely as a concession to the Sorbonne and to the fashionable exegesis of his own day; and, even so, the Sorbonne was too much in the end for the philosophic thinker. He had once in his life at least to make his submission and demand pardon from the offended orthodoxy of the Paris faculty.

The wave of thought and feeling, thus apologetically and tentatively stirred on the unruffled pond of eighteenth century opinion by the startling plop of Buffon's little smooth-cut pebble, soon widened out on every side in concentric circles, and affected with its wash the entire world of biological science in every country. Before the close of the eighteenth century speculation as to the origin of species was rife in all quarters of Europe. In France itself, Geoffroy St. Hilaire, constitutionally cautious and undecided, but wide of view and free from prejudice, came slowly to the conclusion, in 1795, that all species are really derived by modification from one or more primitive types. In Germany, in the very same year, Goethe, with the keen vision of the poet and the calm eye of the philosopher uniquely combined, discerned independently as by a lightning flash the identical idea of the origin of kinds by modification of pre-existent organisms. 'We may assert without hesitation,' says that great nebulous thinker and observer, 'that all the more perfect organic natures, such as fishes, amphibians, birds and mammals, with man at their head, were formed at first on one original type, which still daily changes and modifies its form by propagation.' In England, twelve months earlier, Dr. Erasmus Darwin, Charles Darwin's grandfather (of whom more anon), published his 'Zoonomia,' a treatise on the laws of animal life, in which he not only adopted Buffon's theory of the origin of species by evolution, but also laid down as the chief cause of such development the actions and needs of the animals themselves. According to Dr. Erasmus Darwin, animals came to vary from one another chiefly because they were always altering their habits and voluntarily accommodating themselves to new actions and positions in life. His work produced comparatively little effect upon the world at large in his own time, but it had immense influence upon the next great prophet of evolution, Lamarck, and through Lamarck on Lyell, Charles Darwin, Herbert Spencer, and the modern school of evolutionists generally. We shall consider his views in greater detail when we pass from the spiritual to the physical antecedents of Charles Darwin.

It was in 1801 that Lamarck first gave to the world his epoch-making speculations and suggestions on the origin of species; and from that date to the day of his death, in 1831, the unwearied old philosopher continued to devote his whole time and energy, in blindness and poverty, to the elucidation of this interesting and important subject. A bold, acute, and vigorous thinker, trained in the great school of Diderot and D'Alembert, with something of the vivid Celtic poetic imagination, and a fearless habit of forming his own conclusions irrespective of common or preconceived ideas, Lamarck went to the very root of the matter in the most determined fashion, and openly proclaimed in the face of frowning officialism under the Napoleonic reaction his profound conviction that all species, including man, were descended by modification from one or more primordial forms. In Charles

Darwin's own words, 'He first did the eminent service of arousing attention to the probability of all change, in the organic as well as in the inorganic world, being the result of law and not of miraculous interposition. Lamarck seems to have been chiefly led to his conclusion on the gradual change of species by the difficulty of distinguishing species and varieties, by the almost perfect gradation of forms in certain groups, and by the analogy of domestic productions. With respect to the means of modification, he attributed something to the direct action of the physical conditions of life, something to the crossing of already existing forms, and much to use and disuse, that is, to the effects of habit. To this latter agency he seems to attribute all the beautiful adaptations in nature—such as the long neck of the giraffe for browsing on the branches of trees,' He believed, in short, that animals had largely developed themselves, by functional effort followed by increased powers and abilities.

Lamarck's great work, the 'Philosophie Zoologique,' though opposed by the austere and formal genius of the immortal Cuvier—a reactionary biological conservative and obscurantist, equal to the enormous task of mapping out piecemeal with infinite skill and power the separate provinces of his chosen science, but incapable of taking in all the bearings of the whole field at a single vivid and comprehensive sweep—Lamarck's great work produced a deep and lasting impression upon the entire subsequent course of evolutionary thought in scientific Europe. True, owing to the retrograde tendencies of the First Empire, it caused but little immediate stir at the precise moment of its first publication; but the seed it sowed sank deep, and, lying fallow long in men's minds, bore fruit at last in the next generation with the marvellous fecundity of the germs of genius. Indeed, from the very beginning of the present century, a ferment of inquiry on the subject of creation and evolution was everywhere obvious among speculative thinkers. The profound interest which Goethe took in the dispute on this very subject in the French Académie des Sciences between Cuvier and Geoffroy St. Hilaire, amid the thundering guns of a threatened European convulsion, was but a solitary symptom of the general stir which preceded the gestation and birth of the Darwinian hypothesis. It is impossible to take up any scientific memoirs or treatises of the first half of our own century without seeing at a glance how every mind of high original scientific importance was permeated and disturbed by the fundamental questions aroused, but not fully answered, by Buffon, Lamarck, and Erasmus Darwin. In Lyell's letters and in Agassiz's lectures, in the 'Botanic Journal' and the 'Philosophical Transactions,' in treatises on Madeira beetles and the Australian flora, we find everywhere the thoughts of men profoundly influenced in a thousand directions by this universal evolutionary solvent and leaven.

And while the world of thought was thus seething and moving restlessly before the wave of ideas set in motion by these various independent philosophers, another group of causes in another field was rendering smooth the path beforehand for the future champion of the amended evolutionism. Geology on the one hand and astronomy on the other were making men's minds gradually familiar with the conception of slow natural development, as opposed to immediate and miraculous creation.

The rise of geology had been rapid and brilliant. In the last century it had been almost universally believed that fossil organisms were the relics of submerged and destroyed worlds, strange remnants of successive terrible mundane catastrophes. Cuvier himself, who had rendered immense services to geological science by his almost unerring reconstructions of extinct animals, remained a partisan of the old theory of constant cataclysms and fresh creations throughout his whole life; but Lamarck, here as elsewhere the prophet of the modern uniformitarian concept of nature, had already announced his grand idea that the ordinary process of natural laws sufficed to account for all the phenomena of the earth's crust. In England, William Smith, the ingenious land surveyor, riding up and down on his daily task over the face of the country, became convinced by his observations in the first years of the present century that a fixed order of sequence could everywhere be traced among the various superincumbent geological strata. Modern scientific geology takes its rise from the moment of this luminous and luminiferous discovery. With astonishing rapidity the sequence of strata was everywhere noted, and the succession of characteristic fossils mapped out, with the result of showing, however imperfectly at first, that the history of organic life upon the globe had followed a slow and regular course of constant development. Immediately whole schools of eager workers employed themselves in investigating in separate detail the phenomena of these successive stages of unfolding life. Murchison, fresh from the Peninsular campaign, began to study the dawn of organic history in the gloom of the Silurian and Cambrian epochs. A group of less articulate but not less active workers like Buckland and Mantell performed similar services for the carboniferous, the wealden, and the tertiary deposits. Sedgwick endeavoured to co-ordinate the whole range of then known facts into a single wide and comprehensive survey. De La Beche, Phillips, and Agassiz added their share to the great work of reconstruction. Last of all, among those who were contemporary and all but coeval with Charles Darwin himself, Lyell boldly fought out the battle of 'uniformitarianism,' proving, with all the accumulated weight of his encyclopædic and world-wide knowledge, that every known feature of geological development could be traced to the agency of causes now in action, and illustrated by means of slow secular changes still actually taking place on earth before our very eyes.

The influence of these novel conceptions upon the growth and spread of evolutionary ideas was far-reaching and twofold. In the first place, the discovery of a definite succession of nearly related organic forms, following one another with evident closeness through the various ages, inevitably suggested to every inquiring observer the possibility of their direct descent one from the other. In the second place, the discovery that geological formations were not really separated each from its predecessor by violent revolutions, but were the result of gradual and ordinary changes, discredited the old idea of frequent fresh creations after each catastrophe, and familiarised the minds of men of science with the alternative notion of slow and natural evolutionary processes. The past was seen to be in effect the parent of the present; the present was recognised as the child of the past.

Current astronomical theories also pointed inevitably in the same direction. Kant, whose supereminent fame as a philosopher has almost overshadowed his just claims as a profound thinker in physical science, had already in the third quarter of the eighteenth century arrived at his sublime nebular hypothesis, in which he suggested the possible development of stars, suns, planets, and satellites by the slow contraction of very diffuse and incandescent haze-clouds. This magnificent cosmical conception was seized and adapted by the genius of Laplace in his celestial system, and made familiar through his great work to thinking minds throughout the whole of Europe. In England it was further modified and remodelled by Sir William Herschel, whose period of active investigation coincided in part with Charles Darwin's early boyhood. The bearings of the nebular hypothesis upon the rise of Darwinian evolutionism are by no means remote: the entire modern scientific movement forms, in fact, a single great organic whole, of which the special doctrine of biological development is but a small separate integral part. All the theories and doctrines which go to make it up display the one common trait that they reject the idea of direct creative interposition from without, and attribute the entire existing order of nature to the regular unfolding of one undeviating continuous law.

Yet another factor in the intellectual stir and bustle of the time must needs be mentioned even in so short and cursory a sketch as this of the causes which led to the Darwinian crisis. In 1798, Thomas Malthus, a clergyman of the Church of England, published the first edition of his famous and much-debated 'Essay on the Principle of Population.' Malthus was the first person who ever called public attention to the tendency of population to increase up to the utmost limit of subsistence, as well as to the necessary influence of starvation in checking its further development beyond that point. Though his essay dealt only with the question of reproduction in human societies, it was clear that it possessed innumerable analogies in every domain of animal and vegetable life. The book ran through many successive editions with extraordinary rapidity for a work of its class, it was fiercely attacked and bravely defended, it caused an immense amount of discussion and debate, and besides its marvellous direct influence as a germinal power upon the whole subsequent course of politico-economical and sociological thought, it produced also a remarkable indirect influence on the side current of biological and speculative opinion. In particular, as we shall more fully see hereafter, it had an immediate effect in suggesting to the mind of the great naturalist who forms our present subject the embryo idea of 'natural selection.'

Such then was the intellectual and social world into which, early in the present century, Charles Darwin found himself born. Everywhere around him in his childhood and youth these great but formless evolutionary ideas were brewing and fermenting. The scientific society of his elders and of the contemporaries among whom he grew up was permeated with the leaven of Laplace and of Lamarck, of Hutton and of Herschel. Inquiry was especially everywhere rife as to the origin and nature of specific distinctions among plants and animals. Those who believed in the doctrine of Buffon and of the 'Zoonomia' and those who disbelieved in it, alike, were profoundly interested and agitated in soul by the far-reaching implications of that fundamental problem. On every side evolutionism, in its crude form, was already in the air. Long before Charles Darwin himself published his conclusive 'Origin of Species,' every thinking mind in the world of science, elder and younger, was deeply engaged upon the self-same problem. Lyell and Horner in alternate fits were doubting and debating. Herbert Spencer had already frankly accepted the new idea with the profound conviction of *a priori* reasoning. Agassiz was hesitating and raising difficulties. Treviranus was ardently proclaiming his unflinching adhesion. Oken was spinning in metaphysical Germany his fanciful parodies of the Lamarckian hypothesis. Among the depths of Brazilian forests Bates was reading the story of evolution on the gauze-like wings of tropical butterflies. Under the scanty shade of Malayan palm-trees Wallace was independently spelling out in rude outline the very theory of survival of the fittest, which Charles Darwin himself was simultaneously perfecting and polishing among the memoirs and pamphlets of his English study. Wollaston in Madeira was pointing out the strange adaptations of the curious local snails and beetles. Von Buch in the Canaries was coming to the conclusion that varieties may be slowly changed into permanent species. Lecoq and Von Baer were gradually arriving, one by the botanical route, the other by the embryological, at the same opinion. Before Charles Darwin was twenty, Dean Herbert had declared from the profound depth of his horticultural knowledge that kinds were only mere fixed sports; and Patrick Matthew, in the appendix to a work on 'Naval Timber,' had casually developed, without perceiving its importance, the actual distinctive Darwinian doctrine of natural selection. Robert Chambers published in 1844 his 'Vestiges of Creation,' in which Lamarck's theory was impressed and popularised under a somewhat spoilt and mistaken form: it was not till 1859 that the first edition of the 'Origin of Species' burst like a thunderbolt upon the astonished world of unprepared and unscientific thinkers.

This general attitude of interest and inquiry is of deep importance to the proper comprehension of Charles Darwin's life and work, and that for two distinct reasons. In the first place, the universal stir and deep prying into evolutionary questions which everywhere existed among scientific men in his early days was naturally communicated to a lad born of a scientific family, and inheriting directly in blood and bone the biological tastes and tendencies of Erasmus Darwin. In the second place, the existence of such a deep and wide-spread curiosity as to ultimate origins, and the common prevalence of profound uniformitarian and evolutionary views among philosophers and thinkers, made the acceptance of Charles Darwin's particular theory, when it at last arrived, a comparatively easy and certain matter, because by it the course of organic development was assimilated, on credible grounds, to the course of all other development in general, as then already widely recognised. The first consideration helps us to account in part for the man himself; the second consideration helps us even more to account for the great work which he was enabled in the end so successfully to accomplish.

# CHAPTER II.

## CHARLES DARWIN AND HIS ANTECEDENTS.

From the environment let us turn to the individual; from the world in which the man moved to the man who moved in it, and was in time destined to move it.

Who was he, and whence did he derive his exceptional energy and intellectual panoply?

Erasmus Darwin, the grandfather, the first of the line in whom the distinctive Darwinian strain of intellect overtly displayed itself, was the son of one Robert Darwin, a gentleman of Nottinghamshire, 'a person of curiosity,' with 'a taste for literature and science;' so that for four generations at least, in the paternal line, the peculiar talents of the Darwin family had been highly cultivated in either direction. Robert Darwin was an early member of the Spalding Club, a friend of Stukeley the antiquary, and an embryo geologist, after the fantastic, half-superstitious fashion of his own time. Of his four sons, both Robert, the eldest, and Erasmus, the youngest, were authors and botanists. Erasmus himself was a Cambridge man, and his natural bent of mind and energy led him irresistibly on to the study of medicine. Taking his medical degree at his own university, and afterwards preparing for practice by attending Hunter's lectures in London, besides going through the regular medical course at Edinburgh, the young doctor finally settled down as a physician at Nottingham, whence shortly afterward he removed to Lichfield, then the centre of a famous literary coterie. So large a part of Charles Darwin's remarkable idiosyncrasy was derived by heredity from his paternal grandfather, that it may be worth while to dwell a little here in passing on the character and career of this brilliant precursor of the great evolutionist. Both in the physical and in the spiritual sense, Erasmus Darwin was one among the truest and most genuine ancestors of his grandson Charles.

A powerful, robust, athletic man, in florid health and of temperate habits, yet with the full-blooded tendency of the eighteenth century vividly displayed in his ample face and broad features, Erasmus Darwin bubbled over with irrepressible vivacity, the outward and visible sign of that overflowing energy which forms everywhere one of the most marked determining conditions of high genius. Strong in body and strong in mind, a teetotaler before teetotalism, an abolitionist before the anti-slavery movement, he had a great contempt for weaknesses and prejudices of every sort, and he rose far superior to the age in which he lived in breadth of view and freedom from preconceptions. The eighteenth century considered him, in its cautious, cut-and-dried fashion, a man of singular talent but of remarkably eccentric and unsafe opinions. Unfortunately for his lasting fame, Dr. Darwin was much given to writing poetry; and this poetry, though as ingenious as everything else he did, had a certain false gallop of verse about it which has doomed it to become since Canning's parody a sort of warning beacon against the worst faults of the post-Augustan decadence in the ten-syllabled metre. Nobody now reads the 'Botanic Garden' except either to laugh at its exquisite extravagances, or to wonder at the queer tinsel glitter of its occasional clever rhetorical rhapsodies.

But in his alternative character of philosophic biologist, rejected by the age which swallowed his poetry all applausive, Erasmus Darwin is well worthy of the highest and deepest respect, as a prime founder and early prophet of the evolutionary system. His 'Zoonomia,' 'which, though ingenious, is built upon the most absurd hypothesis'—as men still said only thirty years ago—contains in the germ the whole theory of organic development as understood up to the very moment of the publication of the 'Origin of Species.' In it Dr. Darwin calls attention to 'the great changes introduced into various animals by artificial or accidental cultivation,' a subject afterwards fully elucidated by his greater grandson in his work on 'The Variation of Animals and Plants under Domestication.' He specially notes 'the immense changes of shape and colour' produced by man in rabbits and pigeons, the very species on which Charles Darwin subsequently made some of his most remarkable and interesting observations. More than any previous writer, Erasmus Darwin, with 'prophetic sagacity,' insisted strongly on the essential unity of parent and offspring—a truth which lies at the very base of all modern philosophical biology. 'Owing to the imperfection of language,' wrote the Lichfield doctor nearly a hundred years ago, 'the offspring is termed a new animal, but is in truth a branch or elongation of the parent, since a part of the embryon-animal is or was a part of the parent, and therefore may retain some of the habits of the parent system.' He laid peculiar stress upon the hereditary nature of some acquired properties, such as the muscles of dancers or jugglers, and the diseases incidental to special occupations. Nay, he even anticipated his great descendant in pointing out that varieties are often produced at first as mere 'sports' or accidental variations, as in the case of six-fingered men, five-clawed fowls, or extra-toed cats, and are afterwards handed down by heredity to succeeding generations. Charles Darwin would have added that if these new stray peculiarities happened to prove advantageous to the species they would be naturally favoured in the struggle for existence, while if they proved disadvantageous, or even neutral, they would die out at once or be bred out in the course of a few crosses. That last truth of natural selection was the only cardinal one in the evolutionary system on which Erasmus Darwin did not actually forestall his more famous and greater namesake. For its full perception, the discovery of Malthus had to be collated with the speculations of Buffon.

'When we revolve in our minds,' says the eighteenth century prophet of evolution, 'the great similarity of structure which obtains in all the warm-blooded animals, as well quadrupeds, birds, and amphibious animals, as in mankind; from the mouse and bat to the elephant and whale; one is led to conclude that they have alike been produced from a similar living filament. In some this filament in its advance to maturity has acquired hands and fingers with a fine sense of touch, as in mankind. In others it has acquired claws or talons, as in tigers and eagles. In others, toes with an intervening web or membrane, as in seals and geese. In others it has acquired cloven hoofs, as in cows and swine; and whole hoofs in others, as in the horse: while in the bird kind this original living filament has put forth wings instead of arms or legs, and feathers instead of hair.' This is a very crude form of evolutionism indeed, but it is leading up by gradual stages to the finished and all-sided philosophy of physical life, which at last definitely formulates itself through the mouth of Charles Darwin. We shall see hereafter wherein Erasmus Darwin's conception of development chiefly failed—in attributing evolution for the most part to the exertions and endeavours of the animal itself, rather than to inevitable survival of the fittest among innumerable spontaneous variations—but we must at least conclude our glimpse of his pregnant and suggestive work by quoting its great fundamental *aperçu*:—'As the earth and ocean were probably peopled with vegetable productions long before the existence of animals, and many families of these animals long before other families of them, shall we conjecture that one and the same kind of living filament is and has been the cause of all organic life?'

A few lines from the 'Temple of Nature,' one of Erasmus Darwin's poetic rhapsodies, containing his fully matured views on the origin of living creatures, may be worth reproduction in further elucidation of his philosophical position:—

> 'Organic life beneath the shoreless waves
> Was born, and nursed in ocean's pearly caves;
> First forms minute, unseen by spheric glass.
> Move on the mud, or pierce the watery mass;
> These, as successive generations bloom,
> New powers acquire, and larger limbs assume;
> Whence countless groups of vegetation spring,
> And breathing realms of fin and feet and wing.'

Have we not here the very beginnings of Charles Darwin? Do we not see, in these profound and fundamental suggestions, not merely hints as to the evolution of evolution, but also as to the evolution of the evolutionist?

On the other hand, though Erasmus Darwin defined a fool to his friend Edgeworth as 'a man who never tried an experiment in his life,' he was wanting himself in the rigorous and patient inductive habit which so strikingly distinguished his grandson Charles. That trait, as we shall presently see, the biological chief of the nineteenth century derived in all probability from another root of his genealogical tree. Erasmus Darwin gave us brilliant suggestions rather than cumulative proof: he apologised in his 'Zoonomia' for 'many conjectures not supported by accurate investigation or conclusive experiments,' Such an apology would have been simply impossible to the painstaking spirit of his grandson Charles.

Erasmus Darwin was twice married. His first wife was Mary, daughter of Mr. Charles Howard, of Lichfield, and it was her son, Robert Waring Darwin, who became the father of our hero, Charles. It is fashionable to say, in this and sundry other like cases, that the mental energy skips a generation. People have said so in the case of that intermediate Mendelssohn who was son of Moses Mendelssohn, the philosopher, and father of Felix Bartholdy Mendelssohn, the composer—that mere link in a marvellous chain who was wont to observe of himself in the decline of life, that in his youth he was called the son of the great Mendelssohn, and in his old age the father of the great Mendelssohn. As a matter of fact, one may fairly doubt whether such a case of actual skipping is ever possible in the nature of things. In the particular instance of Robert Waring Darwin at least we may be pretty sure that the distinctive Darwinian strain of genius lay merely latent rather than dormant: that it did not display itself to the world at large, but that it persisted silently as powerful as ever within the remote recesses of the thinking organism. Not every man brings out before men all that is within him. Robert Waring Darwin was a physician at Shrewsbury; and he attained at least sufficient scientific eminence in his own time to become a Fellow of the Royal Society, in days when that honour was certainly not readily conferred upon country doctors of modest reputation. Charles Darwin says of him plainly, 'He was incomparably the most acute observer whom I ever knew.' It may well have been that Robert Darwin lived and died, as his famous son lived for fifty years of his great life, in comparative silence and learned retirement; for we must never forget that if Charles Darwin had only completed the first half century of his laborious existence, he would have been remembered merely as the author of an entertaining work on the voyage of the 'Beagle,' a plausible theory of coral islands, and a learned monograph on the fossil barnacles. During all those years, in fact, he had really done little else than collect material for the work of his lifetime. If we judge men by outward performance only, we may often be greatly mistaken in our estimates: potentiality is wider than actuality; what a man does is never a certain or extreme criterion of what he can do.

The Darwins, indeed, were all a mighty folk, of varied powers and varied attainments. Erasmus's brother, Robert, was the author of a work on botany, which long enjoyed a respectable repute. Of his sons, one, Sir Francis Darwin, was noted as a keen observer of animals; a second, Charles, who died at twenty-one, was already the author of a very valuable medical essay; while the third, Robert, was the Shrewsbury F.R.S., the father of our great evolutionary thinker. And among Charles Darwin's own cousins, one is Mr. Hensleigh Wedgwood, the philologist; a second was the late Sir Henry Holland; and a third is Mr. Francis Galton, the author of that essentially Darwinian book, 'Hereditary Genius.'

Robert Waring Darwin took to himself a wife from another very great and eminent family. He married Susannah Wedgwood, daughter of Josiah Wedgwood, the famous potter; and from these two silent representatives of powerful stocks, Charles Robert Darwin, the father of modern evolutionary biology, was born at Shrewsbury, on February the 12th, 1809. That Wedgwood connection, again, is no mere casual or unimportant incident in the previous life-history of the Darwinian originality; it throws a separate clear light of its own upon the peculiar and admirably compounded idiosyncrasy of Charles Darwin.

A man, indeed, owes on the average quite as much to his mother's as to his father's family. It is a mere unscientific old-world prejudice which makes us for the most part count ancestry in the direct ascending male line alone, to the complete neglect of the equally important maternal pedigree. Prom the biological point of view, at least, every individual is a highly complex compound of hereditary elements, a resultant of numerous converging forces, a meeting place of two great streams of inheritance, each of which is itself similarly made up by the like confluence of innumerable distinct prior tributaries. Between these two it is almost impossible for us accurately to distribute any given individuality. How much Charles Darwin owed to the Darwins, and how much he owed in turn to the Wedgwoods, no man is yet psychologist enough or physiologist enough to say. But that he owed a great deal to either strong and vigorous strain we may even now quite safely take for granted.

The Wedgwood family were 'throwers' by handicraft, superior artisans long settled at Burslem, in the Staffordshire potteries. Josiah, the youngest of thirteen children, lamed by illness in early life, was turned by this happy accident from his primitive task as a 'thrower' to the more artistic and original work of producing ornamental coloured earthenware. Skilful and indefatigable, of indomitable energy and with great powers of forcing his way in life against all obstacles, young Wedgwood rose rapidly by his own unaided exertions to be a master potter, and a manufacturer of the famous unglazed black porcelain. Those were the darkest days of industrial art and decorative handicraft in modern England. Josiah Wedgwood, by his marked originality and force of character, succeeded in turning the current of national taste, and creating among us a new and distinctly higher type of artistic workmanship. His activity, however, was not confined to his art alone, but found itself a hundred other different outlets in the most varied directions. When his potteries needed enlargement to meet the increased demand, he founded for the hands employed upon his works the model industrial village of Etruria. When Brindley began cutting artificial waterways across the broad face of central England, it was in the great potter that he found his chief ally in promoting the construction of the Grand Trunk Canal. Wedgwood, indeed, was a builder of schools and a maker of roads; a chemist and an artist; a friend of Watt and an employer of Flaxman. In short, like Erasmus Darwin, he possessed that prime essential in the character of genius, an immense underlying stock of energy. And with it there went its best concomitant, the 'infinite capacity for taking pains.' Is it not probable that in their joint descendant, the brilliant but discursive and hazardous genius of Erasmus Darwin was balanced and regulated by soberer qualities inherited directly from the profound industry of the painstaking potter? When later on we find Charles Darwin spending hours in noting the successive movements of the tendrils in a plant, or watching for long years the habits and manners of earthworms in flower-pots, may we not reasonably conjecture that he derived no little share of his extraordinary patience, carefulness, and minuteness of handicraft from his mother's father, Josiah Wedgwood?

Such, then, were the two main component elements, paternal and maternal, from which the striking personality of Charles Darwin was no doubt for the most part ultimately built up.

# CHAPTER III.

## EARLY DAYS.

As the Chester express steams out of Shrewsbury station, you see on your left, overhanging the steep bank of Severn, a large, square, substantial-looking house, known as the Mount, the birthplace of the author of the 'Origin of Species.' There, in the comfortable home he had built for himself, Dr. Robert Darwin, the father, lived and worked for fifty years of unobtrusive usefulness. He had studied medicine at Edinburgh and Leyden, and had even travelled a little in Germany, before he settled down in the quiet old Salopian town, where for half a century his portly figure and yellow chaise were familiar objects of the country-side for miles around. Among a literary society which included Coleridge's friends, the Tayleurs, and where Hazlitt listened with delight to the great poet's 'music of the spheres,' in High Street Unitarian Chapel, the Mount kept up with becoming dignity the family traditions of the Darwins and the Wedgwoods as a local centre of sweetness and light.

On February the 12th, 1809, Charles Darwin first saw the light of day in this his father's house at Shrewsbury. Time and place were both propitious. Born in a cultivated scientific family, surrounded from his birth by elevating influences, and secured beforehand from the cramping necessity of earning his own livelihood by his own exertions, the boy was destined to grow up to full maturity in the twenty-one years of slow development that immediately preceded the passing of the first Reform Act. The thunder of the great European upheaval had grown silent at Waterloo when he was barely six years old, and his boyhood was passed amid country sights and sounds during that long period of reconstruction and assimilation which followed the fierce volcanic outburst of the French Revolution. Happy in the opportunity of his birth, he came upon the world eight years after the first publication of Lamarck's remarkable speculations, and for the first twenty-two years of his life he was actually the far younger contemporary of the great French evolutionary philosopher. Eleven years before his arrival upon the scene Malthus had set forth his 'Principle of Population.' Charles Darwin thus entered upon a stage well prepared for him, and he entered it with an idiosyncrasy exactly adapted for making the best of the situation. The soil had been thoroughly turned and dressed beforehand: Charles Darwin's seed had only to fall upon it in order to spring up and bear fruit a hundredfold, in every field of science or speculation.

For it was not biology alone that he was foredoomed to revolutionise, but the whole range of human thought, and perhaps even ultimately of human action.

Is it mere national prejudice which makes one add with congratulatory pleasure that Darwin was born in England, rather than in France, in Germany, or in America? Perhaps so; perhaps not. For the English intellect does indeed seem more capable than most of uniting high speculative ability with high practical skill and experience: and of that union of rare qualities Darwin himself was a most conspicuous example. It is probable that England has produced more of the great organising and systematising intellects than any other modern country.

Among those thinkers in his own line who stood more nearly abreast of Darwin in the matter of age, Lyell was some eleven years his senior, and contributed not a little (though quite unconsciously) by his work and conclusions to the formation of Darwin's own peculiar scientific opinions. The veteran Owen, who still survives him, was nearly five years older than Darwin, and also helped to a great extent in giving form and exactness to his great contemporary's anatomical ideas. Humboldt, who preceded our English naturalist in the matter of time by no less than forty years, might yet almost rank as coeval in some respects, owing to his long and active life, his late maturity, and the very recent date of his greatest and most thought-compelling work, the 'Cosmos' (begun when Humboldt was seventy-five, and finished when he lacked but ten years of his century), in itself a sort of preparation for due acceptance of the Darwinian theories. In fact, as many as fifty years of their joint lives coincided entirely one with the other's. Agassiz antedated Darwin by two years. On the other hand, among the men who most helped on the recognition of Darwin's theories, Hooker and Lewes were his juniors by eight years, Herbert Spencer by eleven, Wallace by thirteen, and Huxley by sixteen. His cousin, Francis Galton, another grandson of Erasmus Darwin, and joint inheritor of the distinctive family biological ply, was born at the same date as Alfred Russell Wallace, thirteen years after Charles Darwin. In such a goodly galaxy of workers was the Darwinian light destined to shine through the middle of the century, as one star excelleth another in glory.

Charles Darwin was the second son: but nature refuses doggedly to acknowledge the custom of primogeniture. His elder brother, Erasmus, a man of mute and inarticulate ability, with a sardonic humour alien to his race, extorted unwonted praise from the critical pen of Thomas Carlyle, who 'for intellect rather preferred him to his brother Charles.' But whatever spark of the Darwinian genius was really innate in Erasmus the Less died with him unacknowledged.

The boy was educated (so they call it) at Shrewsbury Grammar School, under sturdy Sam Butler, afterwards Bishop of Lichfield; and there he picked up so much Latin and Greek as was then considered absolutely essential to the due production of an English gentleman. Happily for the world, having no taste for the classics, he escaped the ordeal with little injury to his individuality. His mother had died while he was still a child, but his father, that 'acute observer,' no doubt taught him to know and love nature. At sixteen he went to Edinburgh University, then rendered famous by a little knot of distinguished professors, and there he remained for two years. Already at school he had made himself notable by his love of collecting—the first nascent symptom of the naturalist bent. He collected everything, shells, eggs, minerals, coins, nay, since postage stamps were then not yet invented, even franks. But at Edinburgh he gave the earliest distinct evidence of his definite scientific tastes by contributing to the local academic society a paper on the floating eggs of the common sea-mat, in which he had even then succeeded in discovering for the first time organs of locomotion. Thence he proceeded to Christ's College, Cambridge. The Darwins were luckily a Cambridge family: luckily, let us say, for had it been otherwise—had young Darwin been distorted from his native bent by Plato and Aristotle, and plunged deep into the mysteries of Barbara and Celarent, as would infallibly have happened to him at the sister university—who can tell how long we might have had to wait in vain for the 'Origin of Species' and the 'Descent of Man'? But Cambridge, which rejoiced already in the glory of Newton, was now to match it by the glory of Darwin. In its academical course, the mathematical wedge had always kept open a dim passage for physical science; and at the exact moment when Darwin was an undergraduate at Christ's—from 1827 to 1831—the university had the advantage of several good scientific teachers, and amongst them one, Professor Henslow, a well-known botanist, who took a special interest in young Darwin's intellectual development. There, too, he met with Sedgwick, Airy, Ramsay, and numerous other men of science, whose intercourse with him must no doubt have contributed largely to mould and form the future cast of his peculiar philosophical idiosyncrasy.

It was to Henslow's influence that Darwin in later years attributed in great part his powerful taste for natural history. But in truth the ascription of such high praise to his early teacher smacks too much of the Darwinian modesty to be accepted at once without demur by the candid critic. The naturalist, like the poet, is born, not made. How much more, then, must this needs be the case with the grandson of Erasmus Darwin and of Josiah Wedgwood? As a matter of fact, already at Edinburgh the lad had loved to spend his days among the sea-beasts and wrack of the Inches in the Firth of Forth; and it was through the instrumentality of his 'brother entomologists' that he first became acquainted with Henslow himself when he removed to Cambridge. The good professor could not make him into a naturalist: inherited tendencies and native energies had done that for him already from his very cradle.

'Doctrina sed vim promovet insitam;' and it was well that Darwin took up at Cambridge with the study of geology as his first love. For geology was then the living and moving science, as astronomy had been in the sixteenth century, and as biology is at the present day—the growing-point, so to speak, of European development, whence all great things might naturally be expected. Moreover, it was and is the central science of the concrete class, having relations with astronomy on the one hand, and with biology on the other; concerned alike with cosmical chances or changes on this side, and with the minutest facts of organic nature on that; the meeting-place and border-land of all the separate branches of study that finally bear upon the complex problems of our human life. No other subject of investigation was so well calculated to rouse Darwin's interest in the ultimate questions of evolution or creation, of sudden cataclysm or gradual growth, of miraculous intervention or slow development. Here, if anywhere, his enigmas were all clearly propounded to him by the inarticulate stony sphinxes; he had only to riddle them out for himself as he went along in after years with the aid of the successive side-lights thrown upon the world by the unconnected lanterns of Lamarck and of Malthus.

Fortunately for us, then, Darwin did not waste his time at Cambridge over the vain and frivolous pursuits of the classical tripos. He preferred to work at his own subjects in his own way, and to leave the short-lived honours of the schools to those who cared for them and for nothing higher. He came out with the *οἱ πολλοί* in 1831, and thenceforth proceeded to study life in the wider university for which his natural inclinations more properly fitted him. The world was all before him where to choose, and he chose that better part which shall not be taken away from him as long as the very memory of science survives.

# CHAPTER IV.

## DARWIN'S WANDER-YEARS.

Scarcely had Darwin taken his pass degree at Cambridge when the great event of his life occurred which, more than anything else perhaps, gave the final direction to his categorical genius in the line it was thenceforth so successfully to follow. In the autumn of 1831, when Darwin was just twenty-two, it was decided by Government to send a ten-gun brig, the 'Beagle,' under command of Captain Fitzroy, to complete the unfinished survey of Patagonia and Tierra del Fuego, to map out the shores of Chili and Peru, to visit several of the Pacific archipelagoes, and to carry a chain of chronometrical measurements round the whole world. This was an essentially scientific expedition, and Captain Fitzroy, afterwards so famous as the meteorological admiral, was a scientific officer of the highest type. He was anxious to be accompanied on his cruise by a competent naturalist who would undertake the collection and preservation of the animals and plants discovered on the voyage, for which purpose he generously offered to give up a share of his own cabin accommodation. Professor Henslow seized upon the opportunity to recommend for the post his promising pupil, young Darwin, 'grandson of the poet.' Darwin gladly volunteered his services without salary, and partly paid his own expenses on condition of being permitted to retain in his own possession the animals and plants he collected on the journey. The 'Beagle' set sail from Devonport on December the 27th, 1831; she returned to Falmouth on October the 2nd, 1836.

That long five years' cruise around the world, the journal of which Darwin has left us in the 'Voyage of the "Beagle,"' proved a marvellous epoch in the great naturalist's quiet career. It left its abiding mark deeply imprinted on all his subsequent life and thinking. Lamarck and Erasmus Darwin were cabinet biologists, who had never beheld with their own eyes the great round world and all that therein is; Charles Darwin had the inestimable privilege of seeing for himself, at first hand, a large part of the entire globe and of the creatures that inhabit it. Even to have caught one passing glimpse of the teeming life of the tropics is in itself an education; to the naturalist it is more, it is a revelation. Our starved little northern fauna and flora, the mere leavings of the vast ice sheets that spread across our zone in the glacial epoch, show us a world depopulated of all its largest, strangest, and fiercest creatures; a world dwarfed in all its component elements, and immensely differing in ten thousand ways from that rich, luxuriant, over-stocked hot-house in which the first great problems of evolution were practically worked out by survival of the fittest. But the tropics preserve for us still in all their jungles something of the tangled, thickly-peopled aspect which our planet must have presented for countless ages in all latitudes before the advent of primæval man. We now know that throughout the greater part of geological time, essentially tropical conditions existed unbroken over the whole surface of the entire earth, from the Antarctic continent to the shores of Greenland; so that some immediate acquaintance at least with the equatorial world is of immense value to the philosophical naturalist for the sake of the analogies it inevitably suggests; and it is a significant fact that almost all those great and fruitful thinkers who in our own time have done good work in the wider combination of biological facts have themselves passed a considerable number of years in investigating the conditions of tropical nature. Europe and England are at the ends of the earth; the tropics are biological head-quarters. The equatorial zone is therefore the true school for the historian of life in its more universal and lasting aspects.

Nor was that all. The particular countries visited by the 'Beagle' during the course of her long and varied cruise happened to be exactly such as were naturally best adapted for bringing out the latent potentialities of Darwin's mind, and suggesting to his active and receptive brain those deep problems of life and its environment which he afterwards wrought out with such subtle skill and such consummate patience in the 'Origin of Species' and the 'Descent of Man.' The Cape de Verdes, and the other Atlantic islands, with their scanty population of plants and animals, composed for the most part of waifs and strays drifted to their barren rocks by ocean currents, or blown out helplessly to sea by heavy winds; Brazil, with its marvellous contrasting wealth of tropical luxuriance and self-strangling fertility, a new province of interminable delights to the soul of the enthusiastic young collector; the South American pampas, with their colossal remains of extinct animals, huge geological precursors of the stunted modern sloths and armadillos that still inhabit the self-same plains; Tierra del Fuego, with its almost Arctic climate, and its glimpses into the secrets of the most degraded savage types; the vast range of the Andes and the Cordilleras, with their volcanic energy and their closely crowded horizontal belts of climatic life; the South Sea Islands, those paradises of the Pacific, Hesperian fables true, alike for the lover of the picturesque and the biological student; Australia, that surviving fragment of an extinct world, with an antiquated fauna whose archaic character still closely recalls the European life of ten million years back in the secondary epoch: all these and many others equally novel and equally instructive passed in long alternating panorama before Darwin's eyes, and left their images deeply photographed for ever after on the lasting tablets of his retentive memory. That was the real great university in which he studied nature and read for his degree. Our evolutionist was now being educated.

Throughout the whole of the journal of this long cruise, which Darwin afterwards published in an enlarged form, it is impossible not to be struck at every turn with the way in which his inquisitive mind again and again recurs to the prime elements of those great problems towards whose solution he afterwards so successfully pointed out the path. The Darwinian ideas are all already there in the germ; the embryo form of the 'Origin of Species' plays in and out on every page with the quaintest elusiveness. We are always just on the very point of catching it; and every now and again we do actually all but catch it in essence and spirit, though ever still its bodily shape persistently evades us. Questions of geographical distribution, of geological continuity, of the influence of climate, of the modifiability of instinct, of the effects of surrounding conditions, absorb the young observer's vivid interest at every step, wherever he lands. He is all unconsciously collecting notes and materials in profuse abundance for his great work; he is thinking in rough outline the new thoughts which are hereafter to revolutionise the thought of humanity.

Five years are a great slice out of a man's life: those five years of ceaseless wandering by sea and land were spent by Charles Darwin in accumulating endless observations and hints for the settlement of the profound fundamental problems in which he was even then so deeply interested. The 'Beagle' sailed from England to the Cape de Verdes, and already, even before she had touched her first land, the young naturalist had observed with interest that the impalpably fine dust which fell on deck contained no less than sixty-seven distinct organic forms, two of them belonging to species peculiar to South America. In some of the dust he found particles of stone so very big that they measured 'above the thousandth of an inch square;' and after this fact, says the keen student, 'one need not be surprised at the diffusion of the far lighter and smaller sporules of cryptogamic plants.' Would Erasmus Darwin have noticed these minute points and their implications one wonders? Probably not. May we not see in the observation partly the hereditary tendencies of Josiah Wedgwood towards minute investigation and accuracy of detail, partly the influence of the scientific time-wave, and the careful training under Professor Henslow? Erasmus Darwin comes before us rather as the brilliant and ingenious amateur, his grandson Charles as the instructed and fully equipped final product of the scientific schools.

At St. Paul's Rocks, once more, a mass of new volcanic peaks rising abruptly from the midst of the Atlantic, the naturalist of the 'Beagle' notes with interest that feather and dirt-feeding and parasitic insects or spiders are the first inhabitants to take up their quarters on recently formed oceanic islands. This problem of the peopling of new lands, indeed, so closely connected with the evolution of new species, necessarily obtruded itself upon his attention again and again during his five years' cruise; and in some cases, especially that of the Galapagos Islands, the curious insular faunas and floras which he observed upon this trip, composed as they were of mere casual straylings from adjacent shores, produced upon his mind a very deep and lasting impression, whose traces one may without difficulty discern on every second page of the 'Origin of Species.'

On the last day of February, 1832, the 'Beagle' came to anchor in the harbour of Bahia, and young Darwin caught sight for the first time of the mutually strangling luxuriance of tropical vegetation. Nowhere on earth are the finest conditions of tropical life more fully realised than in the tangled depths of the great uncleared Brazilian forests, which everywhere gird round like a natural palisade with their impenetrable belt the narrow and laborious clearings of over-mastered man. The rich alluvial silt of mighty river systems, the immemorial manuring of the virgin soil, the fierce energy of an almost equatorial sun, and the universal presence of abundant water, combine to make life in that marvellous region unusually wealthy, varied, and crowded, so that the struggle for existence is there perhaps more directly visible to the seeing eye than in any other known portion of God's universe. 'Delight itself,' says Darwin in his journal, with that naive simplicity which everywhere forms the chief charm of his direct and unaffected literary style—'delight itself is a weak term to express the feelings of a naturalist who for the first time has wandered by himself in a Brazilian forest. The elegance of the grasses, the novelty of the parasitical plants, the beauty of the flowers, the glossy green of the foliage, but above all the general luxuriance of the vegetation, filled me with admiration.' In truth, among those huge buttressed trunks, overhung by the unbroken canopy of foliage on the vast spreading and interlacing branches, festooned with lianas and drooping lichens, or beautified by the pendent alien growth of perfumed orchids, Darwin's mind must indeed have found congenial food for apt reflection, and infinite opportunities for inference and induction. Prom the mere picturesque point of view, indeed, the naturalist enjoys such sights as this a thousand times more truly and profoundly than the mere casual unskilled observer: for it is a shallow, self-flattering mistake of vulgar and narrow minds to suppose that fuller knowledge and clearer insight can destroy or impair the beauty of beautiful objects—as who should imagine that a great painter appreciates the sunset less than a silly boy or a sentimental schoolgirl. As a matter of fact, the naturalist knows and admires a thousand exquisite points of detail in every flower and every insect which only he himself and the true artist can equally delight in. And a keen intellectual and æsthetic joy in the glorious fecundity and loveliness of nature was everywhere present to Darwin's mind. But, beyond and above even that, there was also the architectonic delight of the great organiser in the presence of a noble organised product: the peculiar pleasure felt only by the man in whose broader soul all minor details fall at once into their proper place, as component elements in one great consistent and harmonious whole—a sympathetic pleasure akin to that with which an architect views the interior of Ely and of Lincoln, or a musician listens to the linked harmonies of the 'Messiah' and the 'Creation.' The scheme of nature was now unfolding itself visibly and clearly before Charles Darwin's very eyes.

After eighteen memorable days spent with unceasing delight at Bahia, the 'Beagle' sailed again for Rio, where Darwin stopped for three months, to improve his acquaintance with the extraordinary wealth of the South American fauna and flora. Collecting insects was here his chief occupation, and it is interesting to note even at this early period how his attention was attracted by some of those strange alluring devices on the part of the males for charming their partners which afterwards formed the principal basis for his admirable theory of sexual selection, so fully developed in the 'Descent of Man.' 'Several times,' he says, 'when a pair [of butterflies], probably male and female, were chasing each other in an irregular course, they passed within a few yards of me; and I distinctly heard a clicking noise, similar to that produced by a toothed wheel passing under a spring catch.' In like manner he observed here the instincts of tropical ants, the habits of phosphorescent insects, and the horrid practice of that wasp-like creature, the sphex, which stuffs the clay cells of its larvæ full of half-dead spiders and writhing caterpillars, so stung with devilish avoidance of vital parts as to be left quite paralysed yet still alive, as future food for the developing grubs. Cases like these helped naturally to shake the young biologist's primitive faith in the cheap and crude current theories of universal beneficence, and to introduce that wholesome sceptical reaction against received dogma which is the necessary ground-work and due preparation for all great progressive philosophical thinking.

In July they set sail again for Monte Video, where the important question of climate and vegetation began to interest young Darwin's mind. Uruguay is almost entirely treeless; and this curious phenomenon, in a comparatively moist sub-tropical plain-land, struck him as a remarkable anomaly, and set him speculating on its probable cause. Australia, he remembered, was far more arid, and yet its interior was everywhere covered by whole forests of quaint indigenous gum-trees. Could it be that there were no trees adapted to the climate? As yet, the true causes of geographical distribution had not clearly dawned upon Darwin's mind; but that a young man of twenty-three should seriously busy himself about such problems of ultimate causation at all is in itself a sufficiently pointed and remarkable phenomenon. It was here, too, that he first saw that curious animal, the Tucutuco, a true rodent with the habits of a mole, which is almost always found in a blind condition. With reference to this singular creature, there occurs in his journal one of those interesting anticipatory passages which show the rough workings of the distinctive evolutionary Darwinian concept in its earlier stages. 'Considering the strictly subterranean habits of the Tucutuco,' he writes, 'the blindness, though so common, cannot be a very serious evil; yet it appears strange that any animal should possess an organ frequently subject to be injured. Lamarck would have been delighted with this fact, had he known it, when speculating (probably with more truth than usual with him) on the gradually acquired blindness of the Aspalax, a gnawer living under the ground, and of the Proteus, a reptile living in dark caverns filled with water; in both of which animals the eye is in an almost rudimentary state, and is covered by a tendinous membrane and skin. In the common mole the eye is extraordinarily small but perfect, though many anatomists doubt whether it is connected with the true optic nerve; its vision must certainly be imperfect, though probably useful to the animal when it leaves its burrow. In the Tucutuco, which I believe never comes to the surface of the ground, the eye is rather larger, but often rendered blind and useless, though without apparently causing any inconvenience to the animal: no doubt Lamarck would have said that the Tucutuco is now passing into the state of the Aspalax and Proteus.' The passage is instructive both as showing that Darwin was already familiar with Lamarck's writings, and as pointing out the natural course of his own future development.

For the two years from her arrival at Monte Video, the 'Beagle' was employed in surveying the eastern coast of South America; and Darwin enjoyed unusual opportunities for studying the geology, the zoology, and the botany of the surrounding districts during all that period. It was a suggestive field indeed for the young naturalist. The curious relationship of the gigantic fossil armour-plated animals to the existing armadillo, of the huge megatherium to the modern sloths, and of the colossal ant-eaters to their degenerate descendants at the present day, formed one of the direct inciting causes to the special study which produced at last the 'Origin of Species.' In the Introduction to that immortal work Darwin wrote, some twenty-seven years later, 'When on board H.M.S. "Beagle" as naturalist, I was much struck with certain facts in the distribution of the organic beings inhabiting South America, and in the geological relations of the present to the past inhabitants of that continent. These facts, as will be seen in the latter chapters of this volume, seemed to throw some light on the origin of species—that mystery of mysteries, as it has been called by one of our greatest philosophers.' And in the body of the work itself he refers over and over again to numberless observations made by himself during this period of rapid psychological development—observations on the absence of recent geological formations along the lately upheaved South American coast; on the strange extinction of the horse in La Plata; on the affinities of the extinct and recent species; on the effect of minute individual peculiarities in preserving life under special circumstances; and on the influence of insects and blood-sucking bats in determining the existence of the larger naturalised mammals in parts of Brazil and the Argentine Republic. It was the epoch of wide collection of facts, to be afterwards employed in brilliant generalisations: the materials for the 'Origin of Species' were being slowly accumulated in the numberless pigeon-holes of the Darwinian memory.

Among the facts thus industriously gathered by Darwin in the two years spent on the South American coast were several curious instincts of the cuckoo-like molothrus, of the owl of the Pampas, and of the American ostrich. A few sentences scattered here and there through this part of the 'Naturalist's Journal' may well be extracted in the present place as showing, better than any mere secondhand description could do, the slow germinating process of the 'Origin of Species.' In speaking of the toxodon, that strange extinct South American mammal, the young author remarks acutely that, though in size it equalled the elephant and the megatherium, the structure of its teeth shows it to be closely allied to the ruminants, while several other details link it to the pachyderms, and its aquatic peculiarities of ear and nostril approximate it rather to the manatee and the dugong. 'How wonderfully,' he says, 'are the different orders, at the present time so well separated, blended together in different points of the structure of the toxodon.' We now know that unspecialised ancestral forms always display this close union of peculiarities afterwards separately developed in distinct species of their later descendants.

Still more pregnant with evolutionism in the bud is the prophetic remark about a certain singular group of South American birds, 'This small family is one of those which, from its varied relations to other families, although at present offering only difficulties to the systematic naturalist, ultimately may assist in revealing the grand scheme, common to the present and past ages, on which organised beings have been created.' Of the agouti, once more, that true friend of the desert, Darwin notes that it does not now range as far south as Port St. Julian, though Wood in 1670 found it abundant there; and he asks suggestively, 'What cause can have altered, in a wide, uninhabited, and rarely visited country, the range of an animal like this?' Again, when speaking of the analogies between the extinct camel-like macrauchenia and the modern guanaco, as well as of those between the fossil and living species of South American rodents, he says, with even more prophetic insight, 'This wonderful relationship in the same continent between the dead and the living will, I do not doubt, hereafter throw more light on the appearance of organic beings on our earth, and their disappearance from it, than any other class of facts.' He was himself destined in another thirty years to prove the truth of his own vaticination.

A yet more remarkable passage in the 'Journal of the "Beagle,"' though entered under the account of events observed in the year 1834, must almost certainly have been written somewhat later, and subsequently to Darwin's first reading of Malthus's momentous work, 'The Principle of Population,' which (as we know from his own pen) formed a cardinal point in the great biologist's mental development. It runs as follows in the published journal:[1]—'We do not steadily bear in mind how profoundly ignorant we are of the conditions of existence of every animal; nor do we always remember that some check is constantly preventing the too rapid increase of every organised being left in a state of nature. The supply of food, on an average, remains constant; yet the tendency in every animal to increase by propagation is geometrical, and its surprising effects have nowhere been more astonishingly shown than in the case of the European animals run wild during the last few centuries in America. Every animal in a state of nature regularly breeds; yet in a species long established any great increase in numbers is obviously impossible, and must be checked by some means.' Aut Malthus aut Diabolus. And surely here, if anywhere at all, we tremble on the very verge of natural selection.

It would be impossible to follow young Darwin in detail through his journey to Buenos Ayres, and up the Parana to Santa Fé, which occupied the autumn of 1833. In the succeeding year he visited Patagonia and the Falkland Islands, having previously made his first acquaintance with savage life among the naked Fuegians of the extreme southern point of the continent. Some of these interesting natives, taken to England by Captain Fitzroy on a former visit, had accompanied the 'Beagle' through all her wanderings, and from them Darwin obtained that close insight into the workings of savage human nature which he afterwards utilised with such conspicuous ability in the 'Descent of Man.' Through Magellan's Straits the party made their way up the coasts of Chili, and Darwin had there an opportunity of investigating the geology and biology of the Cordillera. The year 1835 was chiefly spent in that temperate country and in tropical Peru; and as the autumn went on, the 'Beagle' made her way across a belt of the Pacific to the Galapagos archipelago.

Small and unimportant as are those little equatorial islands from the geographical and commercial point of view, they will yet remain for ever classic ground to the biologists of the future from their close connection with the master-problems of the 'Origin of Species.' Here more, perhaps, than anywhere else the naturalist of the 'Beagle' found himself face to face in real earnest with the ultimate questions of creation or evolution. A group of tiny volcanic islets, never joined to any land, nor even united to one another, yet each possessing its own

[1] The full narrative was first given to the world in 1839, some three years after Darwin's return to England, so that much of it evidently represents the results of his maturer thinking and reading on the facts collected during his journey round the world.

special zoological features—the Galapagos roused to an extraordinary degree the irresistible questionings of Darwin's mind. They contain no frogs, and no mammal save a mouse, brought to them, no doubt, by some passing ship. The only insects are beetles, which possess peculiar facilities for being transported in the egg or grub across salt water upon floating logs. There are two kinds of snake, one tortoise, and four lizards; but, in striking contrast to this extreme poverty of terrestrial forms, there are at least fifty-five distinct species of native birds. A few snails complete the list. Now most of these animals, though closely resembling the fauna of Ecuador, the nearest mainland, are specifically distinct; they have varied (as we now know) from their continental types owing to natural selection under the new circumstances in which they have been placed. But Darwin had not yet evolved that potent key to the great riddle of organic existence. He saw the problem, but not its solution. 'Most of the organic productions,' he says plainly, 'are aboriginal creations, found nowhere else; there is even a difference between the inhabitants of the different islands: yet all show a marked relationship with those of America, though separated from that continent by an open space of ocean, between 500 and 600 miles in width.... Considering the small size of these islands, we feel the more astonished at the number of their aboriginal beings, and at their confined range. Seeing every height crowned with its crater, and the boundaries of most of the lava-streams still distinct, we are led to believe that within a period geologically recent the unbroken sea was here spread out. Hence, both in space and time we seem to be brought somewhat nearer to that great fact—that mystery of mysteries—the first appearance of new beings on this earth.' Among the most singular of these zoological facts may be mentioned the existence in the Galapagos archipelago of a genus of gigantic and ugly lizard, the amblyrhyncus, unknown elsewhere, but here assuming the forms of two species, the one marine and the other terrestrial. In minuter points, the differences of fauna and flora between the various islands are simply astounding, so as to compel the idea that each form must necessarily have been developed not merely for the group, but for the special island which it actually inhabits. No wonder that Darwin should say in conclusion, 'One is astonished at the amount of creative force, if such an expression may be used, displayed on these small, barren, and rocky islands; and still more so at its diverse, yet analogous, action on points so near each other.' Here again, in real earnest, the young observer trembles visibly on the very verge of natural selection. In the 'Origin of Species' he makes full use, more than once, of the remarkable facts he observed with so much interest in these tiny isolated oceanic specks of the American galaxy.

From the Galapagos the 'Beagle' steered a straight course for Tahiti, and Darwin then beheld with his own eyes the exquisite beauty of the Polynesian Islands. Thence they sailed for New Zealand, the most truly insular large mass of land in the whole world, supplied accordingly with a fauna and flora of most surprising meagreness and poverty of species. In the woods, our observer noted very few birds, and he remarks with astonishment that so big an island—as large as Great Britain—should not possess a single living indigenous mammal, save a solitary rat of doubtful origin. Australia and Tasmania, with their antiquated and stranded marsupial inhabitants, almost completed the round trip. Keeling Island next afforded a basis for the future famous observations upon coral reefs; and thence by

Mauritius, St. Helena, Ascension, Bahia, Pernambuco, and the beautiful Azores, the 'Beagle' made her way home by slow stages to England, which she reached in safety on October the 2nd, 1836. What an ideal education for the future reconstructor of biological science! He had now all his problems cut and dried, ready to his hand, and he had nothing important left to do—except to sit down quietly in his study, and proceed to solve them. Observation and collection had given him one half the subject-matter of the 'Origin of Species;' reflection and Malthus were to give him the other half. Never had great mind a nobler chance; never, again, had noble chance a great mind better adapted by nature and heredity to make the most of it. The man was not wanting to the opportunity, nor was the opportunity wanting to the man. Organism and environment fell together into perfect harmony; and so, by a lucky combination of circumstances, the secret of the ages was finally wrung from not unwilling nature by the far-seeing and industrious volunteer naturalist of the 'Beagle' expedition.

It would be giving a very false idea of the interests which stirred Charles Darwin's mind during his long five years' voyage, however, if we were to dwell exclusively upon the biological side of his numerous observations on that memorable cruise. Ethnology, geology, oceanic phenomena, the height of the snow-line, the climate of the Antarctic islands, the formation of icebergs, the transport of boulders, the habits and manners engendered by slavery, all almost equally aroused in their own way the young naturalist's vivid interest. Nowhere do we get the faintest trace of narrow specialism; nowhere are we cramped within the restricted horizon of the mere vulgar beetle-hunter and butterfly-catcher. The biologist of the 'Beagle' had taken the whole world of science for his special province. Darwin's mind with all its vastness was not, indeed, profoundly analytical. The task of working out the psychological and metaphysical aspects of evolution fell rather to the great organising and systematising intellect of Herbert Spencer. But within the realm of material fact, and of the widest possible inferences based upon such fact, Darwin's keen and comprehensive spirit ranged freely over the whole illimitable field of nature. 'No one,' says Buckle with unwonted felicity, 'can have a firm grasp of any science if, by confining himself to it, he shuts out the light of analogy. He may, no doubt, work at the details of his subject; he may be useful in adding to its facts; he will never be able to enlarge its philosophy. For the philosophy of every department depends on its connection with other departments, and must therefore be sought at their points of contact. It must be looked for in the place where they touch and coalesce: it lies, not in the centre of each science, but on the confines and margin.' This profound truth Darwin fully and instinctively realised. It was the all-embracing catholicity of his manifold interests that raised him into the greatest pure biologist of all time, and that enabled him to co-ordinate with such splendid results the raw data of so many distinct and separate sciences. And even as early as the days of the cruise in the 'Beagle,' that innate catholicity had already asserted itself in full vigour. Now it is a party of Gauchos throwing the bola that engages for the moment his eager attention; and now again it is a group of shivering Fuegians, standing naked with their long hair streaming in the wind on a snowy promontory of their barren coast. Here he examines the tubular lightning-holes melted in the solid rock of Maldonado by the electric energy; and there he observes the moving boulder-streams that course like torrents down the rugged corries of the Falkland Islands. At one time he works upon the unstudied geology of the South American Pampas; at another, he inspects the now classical lagoon and narrow fringing reef of the Keeling archipelago. Everywhere he sees whatever of most noteworthy in animate or inanimate nature is there to be seen; and everywhere he draws from it innumerable lessons, to be applied hereafter to the special field of study upon which his intense and active energies were finally concentrated. It is not too much to say, indeed, that it was the voyage of the 'Beagle' which gave us in the last resort the 'Origin of Species' and its great fellow the 'Descent of Man.'

# CHAPTER V.

## THE PERIOD OF INCUBATION.

When Charles Darwin landed in England on his return from the voyage of the 'Beagle' he was nearly twenty-eight. When he published the first edition of the 'Origin of Species' he was over fifty. The intermediate years, though much occupied by many minor works of deep specialist scientific importance, were still mainly devoted to collecting material for the one crowning effort of his life, the chief monument of his great co-ordinating and commanding intellect—the settlement of the question of organic evolution.

'There is one thing,' says Professor Fiske, 'which a man of original scientific or philosophical genius in a rightly ordered world should never be called upon to do. He should never be called upon to earn a living; for that is a wretched waste of energy, in which the highest intellectual power is sure to suffer serious detriment, and runs the risk of being frittered away into hopeless ruin.' From this unhappy necessity Charles Darwin, like his predecessor Lyell, was luckily free. He settled down early in a home of his own, and worked away at his own occupations, with no sordid need for earning the day's bread, but with perfect leisure to carry out the great destiny for which the chances of the universe had singled him out. His subsequent history is the history of his wonderful and unique contributions to natural science.

The first thing to be done, of course, was the arrangement and classification of the natural history spoils gathered during the cruise, and the preparation of his own journal of the voyage for publication. The strict scientific results of the trip were described in the 'Zoology of the Voyage of the "Beagle,"' the different parts of which were undertaken by rising men of science of the highest distinction, under Charles Darwin's own editorship. Sir Richard Owen took in hand the fossil mammals; Waterhouse arranged their living allies; Gould discussed the birds, Jenyns the fish, and Bell the amphibians and reptiles. In this vast co-operative publication Darwin thus obtained the assistance of many among the most competent specialists in the England of his day, and learned to understand his own collections by the light thrown upon them from the focussed lamps of the most minute technical learning. As for the journal, it was originally published with the general account of the cruise by Captain Fitzroy in 1839, but was afterwards set forth in a separate form under the title of 'A Naturalist's Voyage Round the World.'

But while Darwin was thus engaged in arranging and classifying the animals and plants he had brought home with him, the germs of those inquiring ideas about the origin of species which we have already observed in his account of the voyage were quickening into fresh life within him. As he ruminated at his leisure over the results of his accumulations, he was beginning to work upon the great problem with the definite and conscious resolution of solving it. 'On my return home, it occurred to me,' he says, 'in 1837, that something might perhaps be made out on this question by patiently accumulating and reflecting on all sorts of facts which could possibly have any bearing on it. After five years' work, I allowed myself to speculate on the subject, and drew up some short notes; these I enlarged in 1844 into a sketch of the conclusions that then seemed to me probable; from that period to the present day (1859) I have steadily pursued the same object. I hope that I may be excused for entering on these personal details, as I give them to show that I have not been hasty in coming to a decision.'

So Darwin wrote at fifty. The words are weighty and well worthy of consideration. They give us in a nutshell the true secret of Darwin's success in compelling the attention and assent of his contemporaries to his completed theory. For speculations and hypotheses like those of Lamarck and Erasmus Darwin, however brilliant and luminous they may be, the hard, dry, scientific mind cares as a rule less than nothing. Men of genius and insight like Goethe and Oken may, indeed, seize greedily upon the pregnant suggestion; their intellects are already attuned by nature to its due reception and assimilation; but the mere butterfly-catchers and plant-hunters of the world, with whom after all rests ultimately the practical acceptance or rejection of such a theory, can only be convinced by long and patient accumulations of facts, by infinite instances and endless examples, by exhaustive surveys of the whole field of nature in a thousand petty details piecemeal. They have to be driven by repeated beating into the right path. Everywhere they fancy they see the loophole of an objection, which must be carefully closed beforehand against them with anticipatory argument, as we close hedges by the wayside against the obtrusive donkey with a cautious bunch of thorny brambles. Even if Charles Darwin had hit upon the fundamental idea of natural selection, and had published it, as Wallace did, in the form of a mere splendid *aperçu*, he would never have revolutionised the world of biology. When the great discovery was actually promulgated, it was easy enough to win the assent of philosophical thinkers like Herbert Spencer; easy enough, even, to gain the ready adhesion of non-biological but kindred minds, like Leslie Stephen's and John Morley's; those might all, perhaps, have been readily convinced by far less heavy and crushing artillery than that so triumphantly marshalled together in the 'Origin of Species.' But in order to command the slow and grudging adhesion of the rank and file of scientific workers, the 'hodmen of science,' as Professor Huxley calls them, it was needful to bring together an imposing array of closely serried facts, to secure every post in the rear before taking a single step onward, and to bring to bear upon every antagonist the exact form of argument with which he was already thoroughly familiar. It was by carefully pursuing these safe and cautious philosophical tactics that Charles Darwin gained his great victory. Where others were pregnant, he was cogent. He met the Dryasdusts of science on their own ground, and he put them fairly to flight with their own weapons. More than that, he brought them all over in the long run as deserters into his own camp, and converted them from doubtful and suspicious foes into warm adherents of the evolutionary banner.

Moreover, fortunately for the world, Darwin's own mind was essentially one of the inductive type. If a great deductive thinker and speculator like Herbert Spencer had hit upon the self-same idea of survival of the fittest, he might have communicated it to a small following of receptive disciples, who would have understood it and accepted it, on *a priori* grounds alone, and gradually passed it on to the grades beneath them; but he would never have touched the slow and cautious elephantine intellect of the masses. The common run of mankind are not deductive; they require to have everything made quite clear to them by example and instance. The English intelligence in particular shows itself as a rule congenitally incapable of appreciating the superior logical certitude of the deductive method. Englishmen will not even believe that the square on the hypotenuse is equal to the squares on the containing sides until they have measured and weighed as well as they are able by rude experimental devices a few selected pieces of rudely shaped rectangular paper. It was a great gain, therefore, that the task of reconstructing the course of organic evolution should fall to the lot of a highly trained and masterly intelligence of the inductive order. Darwin had first to convince himself, and then he could proceed to convince the world. He set about the task with characteristic patience and thoroughness. No man that ever lived possessed in a more remarkable degree than he did the innate capacity for taking trouble. For five years, as a mere preliminary, he accumulated facts in immense variety, and then for the first time and in the vaguest possible way he—'allowed himself to speculate.' That brings us down to the year 1842, when the first notes of the 'Origin of Species' must have been tentatively committed to paper. It was in 1859 that the first edition of the complete work was given to the world. Compare this with the case of Newton, who similarly kept his grand idea of gravitation for many years in embryo, until more exact measurements of the moon's mass and distance should enable him to verify it to his own satisfaction.

One other item of immense importance in the genesis of the full Darwinian doctrine deserves mention here—I mean, the exact moment of time occupied by Charles Darwin in the continuous history of scientific thought. A generation or two earlier, in Erasmus Darwin's days, biology had not yet arrived at the true classification of animals and plants upon an essentially hereditary basis. The Linnæan arrangement, then universally accepted, was wholly artificial in its main features; it distributed species without regard to their fundamental likenesses of structure and organisation. But the natural system of Jussieu and De Candolle, by arranging plants into truly related groups, made possible the proofs of an order of affiliation in the vegetable kingdom; while Cuvier's similar reconstruction of the animal world gave a like foothold to the evolutionary philosopher in the other great department of organic nature. The recognition of kinship between the various members of the same family necessarily preceded the establishment of a regular genealogical theory of life in its entirety.

Though we are here concerned mainly with Charles Darwin the thinker and writer—not with Charles Darwin the husband and father—a few words of explanation as to his private life must necessarily be added at the present point, before we pass on to consider the long, slow, and cautious brewing of that wonderful work, the 'Origin of Species,' Darwin returned home from the voyage of the 'Beagle' at the end of the year 1836. Soon after, he was elected a Fellow of the Royal Society, no doubt through the influence of his friend Lyell, who was quite enthusiastic over his splendid geological investigations on the rate of elevation in the Pampas and the Cordillera. Acting on Lyell's advice, too, he determined to seek no official appointment, but to devote himself entirely for the rest of his life to the pursuit of science. In 1838, at the age of twenty-nine, he read before the Geological Society his paper on the 'Connection of Volcanic Phenomena with the Elevation of Mountain Chains,' when, says Lyell admiringly in a private letter, 'he opened upon De la Beche, Phillips, and others'—the veterans of the science—'his whole battery of the earthquakes and volcanoes of the Andes.' Shortly after, the audacious young man was appointed secretary to the Geological Society, a post which he filled when the voyage of the 'Beagle' was first published in 1839.

In the early part of that same year, the rising naturalist took to himself a wife from one of the houses to which he himself owed no small part of his conspicuous greatness. His choice fell upon his cousin, Miss Emma Wedgwood, daughter of Josiah Wedgwood, of Maer Hall; and, after three years of married life in London, he settled at last at Down House, near Orpington, in Kent, where for the rest of his days he passed his time among his conservatories and his pigeons, his garden and his fowls, with his children growing up quietly beside him, and the great thinking world of London within easy reach of a few minutes' journey. His private means enabled him to live the pleasant life of an English country gentleman, and devote himself unremittingly to the pursuit of science. Ill health, indeed, interfered sadly with his powers of work; but system and patience did wonders during his working days, which were regularly parcelled out between study and recreation, and utilised and economised in the very highest possible degree. Early to bed and early to rise, wandering unseen among the lanes and paths, or riding slowly on his favourite black cob, the great naturalist passed forty years happily and usefully at Down, where all the village knew and loved him. A man of singular simplicity and largeness of heart, Charles Darwin never really learnt to know his own greatness. And that charming innocence and ignorance of his real value made the value itself all the greater. His moral qualities, indeed, were no less admirable and unique in their way than his intellectual faculties. To that charming candour and delightful unostentatiousness which everybody must have noticed in his published writings, he united in private life a kindliness of disposition, a width of sympathy, and a ready generosity which made him as much beloved by his friends as he was admired and respected by all Europe. The very servants who came beneath his roof stopped there for the most part during their whole lifetime. In his earlier years at Down, the quiet Kentish home was constantly enlivened by the visits of men like Lyell, Huxley, Hooker, Lubbock, and Wollaston. During his later days, it was the Mecca of a world-wide scientific and philosophic pilgrimage, where all the greatest men our age has produced sought at times the rare honour of sitting before the face of the immortal master. But to the very last Darwin himself never seemed to discover that he was anything more than just an average man of science among his natural peers.

Shortly after Darwin went to Down he began one long and memorable experiment, which in itself casts a flood of light upon his patient and painstaking method of inquiry. Two years before, he had read at the Geological Society a paper on the 'Formation of Mould,' which more than thirty years later he expanded into his famous treatise on the 'Action of Earthworms.' His uncle and father-in-law, Josiah Wedgwood, suggested to him that the apparent sinking of stones on the surface might really be due to earthworm castings. So, as soon as he had some land of his own to experiment upon, he began, in 1842, to spread broken chalk over a field at Down, in which, twenty-nine years later, in 1871, a trench was dug to test the results. What other naturalist ever waited so long and so patiently to discover the upshot of a single experiment? Is it wonderful that a man who worked like that should succeed, not by faith but by logical power, in removing mountains?

Unfortunately, we do not know the exact date when Darwin first read Malthus. But that the perusal of that remarkable book formed a crisis and turning-point in his mental development we know from his own distinct statement in a letter to Haeckel, prefixed to the brilliant German evolutionist's 'History of Creation.' 'It seemed to me probable,' says Darwin, speaking of his own early development, 'that allied species were descended from a common ancestor. But during several years I could not conceive how each form could have been modified so as to become admirably adapted to its place in nature. I began therefore to study domesticated animals and cultivated plants, and after a time perceived that man's power of selecting and breeding from certain individuals was the most powerful of all means in the production of new races. Having attended to the habits of animals and their relations to the surrounding conditions, I was able to realise the severe struggle for existence to which all organisms are subjected; and my geological observations had allowed me to appreciate to a certain extent the duration of past geological periods. With my mind thus prepared I fortunately happened to read Malthus's "Essay on Population" and the idea of natural selection through the struggle for existence at once occurred to me. Of all the subordinate points in the theory, the last which I understood was the cause of the tendency in the descendants from a common progenitor to diverge in character.'

It is impossible, indeed, to overrate the importance of Malthus, viewed as a schoolmaster to bring men to Darwin, and to bring Darwin himself to the truth. Without the 'Essay on the Principle of Population' it is quite conceivable that we should never have had the 'Origin of Species' or the 'Descent of Man.'

At the same time, Darwin had not been idle in other departments of scientific work. Side by side with his collections for his final effort he had been busy on his valuable treatise upon Coral Reefs, in which he proved, mainly from his own observations on the Keeling archipelago, that atolls owe their origin to a subsidence of the supporting ocean-floor, the rate of upward growth of the reefs keeping pace on the whole with the gradual depression of the sea-bottom. 'No more admirable example of scientific method,' says Professor Geikie forty years later, 'was ever given to the world; and even if he had written nothing else, this treatise alone would have placed Darwin in the very front of investigators of nature.' But, from our present psychological and historical point of view, as a moment in the development of Darwin's influence, and therefore of the evolutionary impulse in general, it possesses a still greater and more profound importance, because the work in which the theory is unfolded forms a perfect masterpiece of thorough and comprehensive inductive method, and gained for its author a well-deserved reputation as a sound and sober scientific inquirer. The acquisition of such a reputation, afterwards increased by the publication of the monograph on the Family Cirripedia (in 1851), proved of immense use to Charles Darwin in the fierce battle which was to rage around the unconscious body of the 'Origin of Species.' To be 'sound' is everywhere of incalculable value; to have approved oneself to the slow and cautious intelligence of the Philistine classes is a mighty spear and shield for a strong man; but in England, and above all in scientific England, it is absolutely indispensable to the thinker who would accomplish any great revolution. Soundness is to the world of science what respectability is to the world of business—the *sine qua non* for successfully gaining even a hearing from established personages.

To read the book on Coral Reefs is indeed to take a lesson of the deepest value in applied inductive canons. Every fact is duly marshalled: every conclusion is drawn by the truest and most legitimate process from careful observation or crucial experiment. Bit by bit, Darwin shows most admirably that, through gradual submergence, fringing reefs are developed into barrier-reefs, and these again into atolls or lagoon islands; and incidentally he throws a vivid light on the slow secular movements upward or downward for ever taking place in the world's crust. But the value of the work as a geological record, great as it is, is as nothing compared with its value as a training exercise in inductive logic. Darwin was now learning by experience how to use his own immense powers.

Meanwhile, the environment too had been gradually moving. In 1832, the year after young Darwin set out upon his cruise, Lyell published the first edition of his 'Principles of Geology,' establishing once for all the uniformitarian concept of that branch of science. In 1836, the year when he returned, Rafinesque, in his 'New Flora of North America,' had accepted within certain cramping limits the idea that 'all species might once have been varieties, and that many varieties are gradually becoming species by assuming constant and peculiar characters.' Haldeman in Boston, and Grant at University College, London, were teaching from their professorial chairs the self-same novel and revolutionary doctrine. At last, in 1844, Robert Chambers published anonymously his famous and much-debated 'Vestiges of Creation,' which brought down the question of evolution *versus* creation from the senate of *savants* to the arena of the mere general public, and set up at once a universal fever of inquiry into the mysterious question of the origin of species. Chambers himself was a man rather of general knowledge and some native philosophical insight than of any marked scientific accuracy or depth. His work in its original form displayed comparatively little acquaintance with the vast groundwork of the question at issue—zoological, botanical, geological, and so forth—and in Charles Darwin's own opinion showed 'a great want of scientific caution.' But its graphic style, its vivid picturesqueness, and to the world at large the startling novelty of its brilliant and piquant suggestions, made it burst at once into an unwonted popularity for a work of so distinctly philosophical a character. In nine years it leaped rapidly through no less than ten successive editions, and remained until the publication of the 'Origin of Species' the chief authoritative exponent in England of the still struggling evolutionary principle.

The 'Vestiges of Creation' may be succinctly described as Lamarck and water, the watery element being due in part to the unnecessary obtrusion (*more Scotico*) of a metaphysical and theological principle into the physical universe. Chambers himself, in his latest edition (before the book was finally killed by the advent of Darwinism), thus briefly describes his main concepts: 'The several series of animated beings, from the simplest and oldest up to the highest and most recent, are, under the providence of God, the results, *first,* of an impulse which has been imparted to the forms of life, advancing them, in definite times, by generation, through grades of organisation, terminating in the highest dicotyledons and vertebrata, these grades being few in number, and generally marked by intervals of organic character, which we find to be a practical difficulty in ascertaining affinities; *second,* of another impulse connected with the vital forces, tending, in the course of generations, to modify organic structures in accordance with external circumstances, as food, the nature of the habitat, and the meteoric agencies.' Now it is clear at once that these two supposed 'impulses' are really quite miraculous in their essence. They do not help us at all to a distinct physical and realisable conception of any natural agency whereby species became differentiated one from the other. They lay the whole burden of species-making upon a single primordial supernatural impetus, imparted to the first living germ by the will of the Creator, and acting ever since continuously it is true, but none the less miraculously for all that. For many creations Chambers substitutes one single long creative nisus: where Darwin saw natural selection, his Scotch predecessor saw a *deus ex machina,* helping on the course of organic development by a constant but unseen interference from above. He supposed evolution to be predetermined by some intrinsic and externally implanted proclivity. In short, Chambers's theory is Lamarck's theologised, and spoilt in the process.

The book had nevertheless a most prodigious and perfectly unprecedented success. The secret of its authorship was keenly debated and jealously kept. The most ridiculous surmises as to its anonymous origin were everywhere afloat. Some attributed it to Thackeray, and some to Prince Albert, some to Lyell, some to Sir John Herschel, and some to Charles Darwin himself. Obscurantists thought it a wicked book; 'intellectual' people thought it an advanced book. As a matter of fact it was neither the one nor the other. It was just a pale and colourless transcript of the old familiar teleological Lamarckism. Yet it did good in its generation. The public at large were induced by its ephemeral vogue to interest themselves in a question to which they had never previously given even a passing thought, though more practised biologists of evolutionary tendencies were grieved at heart that evolution should first have been popularly presented to the English world under so unscientific, garbled, and mutilated a form. From the philosophic side, Herbert Spencer found 'this ascription of organic evolution to some aptitude naturally possessed by organisms or miraculously imposed upon them' to be 'one of those explanations which explain nothing—a shaping of ignorance into the semblance of knowledge. The cause assigned,' he says, 'is not a true cause—not a cause assimilable to known causes—not a cause that can be anywhere shown to produce analogous effects. It is a cause unrepresentable in thought: one of those illegitimate symbolic conceptions which cannot by any mental process be elaborated into a real conception.' From the scientific side, on the other hand, Darwin felt sadly the inaccuracy and want of profound technical knowledge everywhere displayed by the anonymous author. These things might naturally cause the enemy to blaspheme. No worse calamity, indeed, can happen to a great truth than for its defence to be intrusted to inefficient hands. Nevertheless, long after, in the 'Origin of Species,' the great naturalist wrote with generous appreciation of the 'Vestiges of Creation,' 'In my own opinion it has done excellent service in this country in calling attention to the subject, in removing prejudice, and in thus preparing the ground for the reception of analogous views.'

Still Darwin gave no sign. A flaccid, cartilaginous, unphilosophic evolutionism had full possession of the field for the moment, and claimed, as it were, to be the genuine representative of the young and vigorous biological creed, while he himself was in truth the real heir to all the honours of the situation. He was in possession of the master-key which alone could unlock the bars that opposed the progress of evolution, and still he waited. He could afford to wait. He was diligently collecting, amassing, investigating; eagerly reading every new systematic work, every book of travels, every scientific journal, every record of sport, or exploration, or discovery, to extract from the dead mass of undigested fact whatever item of implicit value might swell the definite co-ordinated series of notes in his own commonplace books for the now distinctly contemplated 'Origin of Species.' His way was to make all sure behind him, to summon up all his facts in irresistible array, and never to set out upon a public progress until he was secure against all possible attacks of the ever-watchful and alert enemy in the rear. Few men would have had strength of mind enough to resist the temptation offered by the publication of the 'Vestiges of Creation,' and the extraordinary success attained by so flabby a presentation of the evolutionary case: Darwin resisted it, and he did wisely.

We may, however, take it for granted, I doubt not, that it was the appearance and success of Chambers's invertebrate book which induced Darwin, in 1844 (the year of its publication), to enlarge his short notes 'into a sketch of the conclusions which then seemed to him probable.' This sketch he showed to Dr. (now Sir Joseph) Hooker, no doubt as a precaution to ensure his own claim of priority against any future possible competitor. And having thus eased his mind for the moment, he continued to observe, to read, to devour 'Transactions,' to collate instances, with indefatigable persistence for fifteen years longer. If any man mentally measures out fifteen years of his own life, and bethinks him of how long a space it seems when thus deliberately pictured, he will be able to realise a little more definitely—but only a little—how profound was the patience, the self-denial, the single-mindedness of Darwin's intense search after the ultimate truths of natural science.

What was the sketch that he thus committed to paper in 1844, and submitted to the judgment of his friend Hooker? It was the germ of the theory of natural selection. According to that theory, organic development is due to the survival of the fittest among innumerable variations, good, bad, and indifferent, from one or more parent stocks. Darwin's reading of Malthus had suggested to him (apparently as early as the date of publication of the 'Naturalist's Journal') the idea that every species of plant and animal must always be producing a far greater number of seeds, eggs, germs, or young offspring than could possibly be needed for the maintenance of the average number of the species. Of these young, by far the greater number must always perish from generation to generation, for want of space, of food, of air, of raw material. The survivors in each brood must be those naturally best adapted for survival. The many would be eaten, starved, overrun, or crowded out; the few that survive would be those that possessed any special means of defence against aggressors, any special advantage for escaping starvation, any special protection against overrunning or overcrowding foes. Animals and plants, Darwin found on inquiry and investigation, tended to vary under diverse circumstances from the parent or parents that originally produced them. These variations were usually infinitesimal in amount, but sometimes more considerable or even striking. If any particular variation tended in any way to preserve the life of the creatures that exhibited it, beyond the average of their like competitors, that variation would in the long run survive, and the individuals that possessed it, being thus favoured in the struggle for existence, would replace the less adapted form from which they sprang. Darwinism is Malthusianism on the large scale: it is the application of the calculus of population to the wide facts of universal life.

In one sense, indeed, it may be said that, given Malthus on the one hand and the Lamarckian evolutionism on the other, some great man somewhere must sooner or later, almost of necessity, have combined the two, and hit out the doctrine of natural selection as we actually know it. Quite so; but then the point is just this: Darwin *was* the great man in question; he *did* the work which in the very essence of things some such great man was naturally and inevitably predestined to do. You can always easily manage to get on without any particular great man, provided, of course, you have ready to hand another equally able great man by whom to replace him in the scheme of existence. But how many ordinary naturalists possess the width of mind and universality of interest which would prompt them to read, mark, learn, and inwardly digest a politico-economical treatise of the calibre of Malthus? How many, having done so, have the keenness of vision to perceive the ensuing biological implications? How many, having seen them, have the skill and the patience to work up the infinite chaos of botanical and zoological detail into the far-reaching generalisations of the 'Origin of Species'? Merely to have caught at the grand idea is in itself no small achievement; others did so and deserve all honour for their insight; but to flesh it out with all the minute care and conclusive force of Darwin's masterpiece is a thousand times a greater and nobler monument of human endeavour.

During the fifteen years from 1844 to 1859, however, Darwin's pen was by no means idle. In the first-named year he published his 'Geological Observations on Volcanic Islands'—part of the 'Beagle' exploration series; in 1846 he followed this up by his 'Geological Observations on South America;' in 1851 he gave to the world his monograph on 'Recent Barnacles;' and in 1853, his treatise on the fossil species of the same family. But all these works of restricted interest remained always subsidiary to the one great central task of his entire lifetime, the preparation of his projected volume on the Origin of Species.

All through the middle decades of the century Darwin continued to labour at his vast accumulation of illustrative facts; and side by side with his continuous toil, outside opinion kept paving the way for the final acceptance of his lucid ideas. The public was buying and reading all the time its ten editions of the 'Vestiges of Creation.' It was slowly digesting Lyell's 'Principles of Geology,' in which the old cataclysmic theories were featly demolished, and the uniformitarian conception of a past gradually and insensibly merging into the present was conclusively established. It was getting accustomed to statements like those of the younger St. Hilaire, in 1850, that specific characters may be modified by changes in the environing conditions, and that the modifications thus produced may often be of generic value—may make a difference so great that we must regard the product not merely as belonging to a distinct species, but even to a distinct genus or higher kind. In 1852 Herbert Spencer published in the 'Leader' his remarkable essay, contrasting the theories of creation and evolution, as applied to organic beings, with all the biting force of his profound intelligence; and in 1855, the same encyclopædic philosopher put forth the first rough sketch of his 'Principles of Psychology,' in which he took the lead in treating the phenomena of mind from the point of view of gradual development. In that extraordinary work, the philosopher of evolution traced the origin of all mental powers and faculties by slow gradations from the very simplest subjective elements. The 'Principles of Psychology' preceded the 'Origin of Species' by nearly five years; the first collected volume of Mr. Spencer's essays preceded Darwin's work by some twelve months. Baden-Powell's essay on the 'Philosophy of Creation' (much debated and condemned in ecclesiastical circles), and Professor Owen's somewhat contradictory utterances on the nature of types and archetypal ideas, also helped to keep alive interest in the problem of origins up to the very moment of the final appearance of Darwin's great and splendid solution.

It is interesting during these intermediate years to watch from time to time the occasional side-hints of Darwin's activity and of the interest it aroused among his scientific contemporaries. In 1854, for example, Sir Charles Lyell notes, after an evening at Darwin's, how Sir Joseph Hooker astonished him with an account of that strange orchid, Catasetum, which bears three totally distinct kinds of flowers on the same plant; 'It will figure,' he says, 'in C. Darwin's book on species, with many other "ugly facts," as Hooker, clinging like me to the orthodox faith, calls these and other abnormal vagaries.' On a similar occasion, a little later, Lyell asks, after meeting 'Huxley, Hooker, and Wollaston at Darwin's,' 'After all, did we not come from an ourang?' Last of all, in 1857, Darwin himself writes an anticipatory letter to his American friend, Asa Gray, in which he mentions 'six points'—the cardinal conceptions of the 'Origin of Species.' His book is now fairly under weigh; he speaks of it himself to acquaintance and correspondents as an acknowledged project.

Events were growing ripe for the birth. A lucky accident precipitated its parturition in the course of the year 1858.

# CHAPTER VI.

## 'THE ORIGIN OF SPECIES.'

The accident came in this wise.

Alfred Russel Wallace, a young Welsh biologist, went out at twenty-four, in 1848, to the Amazons River, in company with Bates (the author of 'The Naturalist on the Amazons'), to collect birds and butterflies, and to study tropical life in the richest region of equatorial America. Like all other higher zoologists of their time, the two young explorers were deeply interested in the profound questions of origin and metamorphosis, and of geographical distribution, and in the letters that passed between them before they started they avowed to one another that the object of their quest was a solution of the pressing biological enigma of creation or evolution. Starting with fresh hopes and a few pounds in pocket, on an old, worn-out, and unseaworthy slave-trader, they often discussed these deep problems of life and nature together upon the Sargasso sea, or among the palms and lianas of the Brazilian woodlands. The air was thick with whiffs and foretastes of evolutionism, and the two budding naturalists of the Amazons expedition had inhaled them eagerly with every breath. They saw among the mimicking organisms of that equatorial zone strange puzzles to engage their deepest attention; they recognised in the veins and spots that diversified the filmy membranes of insects' wings the hieroglyphs of nature, writing as on a tablet for them to decipher the story of the slow modification of species. In 1852—the year when Herbert Spencer in England published his essay on the 'Development Hypothesis,' and when Naudin in France put forth his bold and able paper on the 'Origin of Species'—Wallace once more returned to Europe, and gave to the world his interesting 'Travels on the Amazons and the Rio Negro.' Two years later the indefatigable traveller set out a second time on a voyage of tropical exploration, among the islands of the Malay archipelago, and for eight years he wandered about in Malay huts and remote islets, gathering in solitude and isolation the enormous store of minute facts which he afterwards lavished with so prodigal a hand upon 'Tropical Nature,' and the 'Geographical Distribution of Animals.'

While Wallace was still at Amboyna, he sent home in 1858 a striking memoir, addressed to Darwin, with a request that he would forward it to Sir Charles Lyell, for presentation to the Linnean Society. Darwin opened and read his brother naturalist's paper, and found to his surprise that it contained his own theory of natural selection, not worked out in detail, as he himself was working it out, but still complete in spirit and essence, with no important portion of the central idea lacking to its full rotundity of conception. A jealous man would have thrown obstacles in the way of publication; but both Darwin and Wallace were born superior to the meannesses of jealousy. The elder naturalist commended his young rival's paper at once to Sir Charles Lyell, who sent it on immediately to the Linnean Society.

But Sir Charles Lyell and Sir Joseph Hooker, both of whom knew of Darwin's work, thought it advisable that he should publish, in the 'Journal' of the Society, a few extracts from his own manuscripts, side by side with Wallace's paper. Darwin, therefore, selected some essential passages for the purpose from his own long-gathered and voluminous notes, and the two contributions were read together before the Society on July the 1st, 1858. That double communication marks the date of birth of modern evolutionism. It is to the eternal credit of both thinkers that each accepted his own true position with regard to the great discovery in perfect sincerity. The elder naturalist never strove for a moment to press his own claim to priority against the younger: the younger, with singular generosity and courtesy, waived his own claim to divide the honours of discovery in favour of the elder. Not one word save words of fraternal admiration and cordial appreciation ever passed the lips of either with regard to the other.

The distinctive notion of natural selection, indeed, like all true and fruitful ideas, had more than once flashed for a moment across the penetrating mind of more than one independent investigator. As early as 1813, Dr. Wells, the famous author of the theory of dew, applied that particular conception to the single case of the production of special races among mankind.

'Of the accidental varieties of man, which would occur among the first few and scattered inhabitants of the middle regions of Africa,' he wrote, 'some one would be better fitted than the others to bear the diseases of the country. This race would consequently multiply, while the others would decrease; not only from their inability to sustain the attacks of disease, but from their incapacity of contending with their more vigorous neighbours.... The same disposition to form varieties still existing, a darker and a darker race would in the course of time occur; and as the darkest would be the best fitted for the climate, this would at last become the most prevalent, if not the only race in the country.' Here we have not merely the radical concept of natural selection, but also the subordinate idea of its exertion upon what Darwin calls 'spontaneous variations.' What is wanting in the paper is the application of the faintly descried law to the facts and circumstances of general biology: Wells saw only a particular instance, where Darwin and Wallace more vividly perceived a universal principle. Again, in 1831, Mr. Patrick Matthew in that singular appendix to his book on naval timber actually enunciates the same idea, applied this time to the whole of nature, in words sometimes almost identical with Darwin's own. 'As nature in all her modifications of life,' says this unconscious discoverer, 'has a power of increase far beyond what is needed to supply the place of what falls by Time's decay, those individuals who possess not the requisite strength, swiftness, hardihood, or cunning, fall prematurely without reproducing—either a prey to their natural devourers, or sinking under disease, generally induced by want of nourishment, their place being occupied by the more perfect of their own kind, who are pressing on the means of existence.... The self-regulating adaptive disposition of organised life may, in part, be traced to the extreme fecundity of nature, who, as before stated, has in all the varieties of her offspring a prolific power much beyond (in many cases a thousandfold) what is necessary to fill up the vacancies caused by senile decay. As the field of existence is limited and preoccupied, it is only the hardier, more robust, better-suited-to-circumstance individuals, who are able to struggle forward to maturity, these inhabiting only the situations to which they have superior adaptation and greater power of occupancy than any other kind; the weaker and less circumstance-suited being prematurely destroyed. This principle is in constant action; it regulates the colour, the figure, the capacities, and instincts; those individuals in each species whose colour and covering are best suited to concealment or protection from enemies, or defence from inclemencies and vicissitudes of climate, whose figure is best accommodated to health, strength, defence, and support; whose capacities and instincts can best regulate the physical energies to self-advantage according to circumstances—in such immense waste of primary and youthful life those only come forward to maturity from the strict ordeal by which nature tests their adaptation to her standard of perfection and fitness to continue their kind by reproduction.' Of the ideas expressed in these paragraphs, and others which preceded them, Darwin himself rightly observes, 'He gives precisely the same view on the origin of species as that propounded by Mr. Wallace and myself. He clearly saw the full force of the principle of natural selection.'

In 1852, once more, so eminent and confirmed an evolutionist as Mr. Herbert Spencer himself had hit upon a glimpse of the same great truth, strange to say without perceiving the width and scope of its implications. 'All mankind,' he wrote in that year in an essay on population in the 'Westminster Review,' 'in turn subject themselves more or less to the discipline described; they either may or may not advance under it; but, in the nature of things, only those who *do* advance under it eventually survive. For, necessarily, families and races whom this increasing difficulty of getting a living which excess of fertility entails does not stimulate to improvements in production.... are on the high road to extinction; and must ultimately be supplanted by those whom the pressure does so stimulate.... And here, indeed, without further illustration, it will be seen that premature death, under all its forms, and from all its causes, cannot fail to work in the same direction. For as those prematurely carried off must, in the average of cases, be those in whom the power of self-preservation is the least, it unavoidably follows that those left behind to continue the race must be those in whom the power of self-preservation is the greatest, must be the select of their generation.' In this striking pre-Darwinian passage we have a partial perception of what Mr. Spencer afterwards described as the survival of the fittest; but, as our great philosopher himself remarks, it 'shows how near one may be to a great generalisation without seeing it.' For not only does Mr. Spencer, like Wells before him, limit the application of the principle to the case of humanity; but, unlike Wells, he overlooks the all-important factor of spontaneous variation, and the power of natural selection, acting upon such, to produce specific and generic divergences of structure. In short, in his own words, the paragraph 'contains merely a passing recognition of the selective process, and indicates no suspicion of the enormous range of its effects, or of the conditions under which a large part of its effects are produced.' On the other hand, it must be noted that both Spencer and Matthew, like Darwin himself, based their ideas largely upon the Malthusian principle, and thus held the two true keys of the situation fairly within their unconscious hands.

Frankly to recognise these various foreshadowings of the distinctive Darwinian theory of natural selection is not in any way to undermine the foundations of Charles Darwin's own real and exceptional greatness. On the contrary, the mere fact that his views were so far anticipated by Wells, Matthew, Spencer, and others, and were simultaneously arrived at across half the globe by the independent intellect of Alfred Russel Wallace, is in itself the very best proof and finest criterion of Charles Darwin's genuine apostleship. No truly grand and fruitful idea was ever yet the sole property of a single originator. Great discoveries, says an acute critic, must always be concerned with some problem of the time which many of the world's foremost minds are just then cudgelling their active brains about. It was so with the discovery of the differential calculus, and of the planet Neptune; with the interpretation of the Egyptian hieroglyphics, and of the cuneiform inscriptions; with the undulatory theory of light, with the mechanical equivalent of heat, with the doctrine of the correlation and conservation of energies, with the invention of the steam engine, the locomotive, the telegraph and the telephone; with the nebular hypothesis, and with spectrum analysis. It was so, too, with the evolutionary movement. The fertile upturning of virgin sod in the biological field which produced Darwin's forerunners, as regards the idea of descent with modification, in the persons of Buffon, Lamarck, and Erasmus Darwin, necessarily produced a little later, under the fresh impetus of the Malthusian conception, his forerunners or coadjutors, as regards the idea of natural selection, in the persons of Wells, Matthew, and Wallace. It was Darwin's task to recognise the universal, where Wells and Spencer had seen only the particular; to build up a vast and irresistible inductive system, where Matthew and Wallace had but thrown out a pregnant hint of wonderful *a priori* interest and suggestiveness. It is one thing to draw out the idea of a campaign, another thing to carry it to a successful conclusion; one thing rudely to sketch a ground-plan, another thing finally to pile aloft to the sky the front of an august and imposing fabric.

As soon as the papers at the Linnean had been read and printed, Darwin set to work in real earnest to bring out the first instalment of his great work. That instalment was the 'Origin of Species.' The first edition was ready for the public on November the 24th, 1859.

In his own mind Darwin regarded that immortal work merely in the light of an abstract of his projected volumes. So immense were his collections and so voluminous his notes that the 'Origin of Species' itself seemed to him like a mere small portion of the contemplated publication. And indeed he did ultimately work out several other portions of his original plan in his detailed treatises on the Variation of Animals and Plants under Domestication, on the Effects of Cross and Self-Fertilisation, and on the Descent of Man and Sexual Selection. But the immense and unexpected vogue of his first volume, the almost immediate revolution which it caused in biological and general opinion, and the all but universal adhesion to his views of all the greatest and most rising naturalists, to a great extent saved him the trouble of carrying out in full the task he had originally contemplated as necessary. Younger and less occupied labourers took part of the work off their leader's hands; the great chief was left to prosecute his special researches in some special lines, and was relieved from the necessity of further proving in minuter detail what he had already proved with sufficient cogency to convince all but the wilfully blind or the hopelessly stupid.

The extraordinary and unprecedented success of the 'Origin of Species' is the truest test of the advance it made upon all previous evolutionary theorising. Those who had never been convinced before were now convinced by sheer force of reasoning; those who believed and those who wavered had their faith confirmed into something like the reposeful calm of absolute certitude.

Let us consider, therefore, what exactly were the additions which Charles Darwin offered in his epoch-making work to the pre-existing conceptions of evolutionists.

In 1852, seven years before the publication of Darwin's masterpiece, Mr. Herbert Spencer wrote as follows in an essay in the 'Leader' on creation and evolution. The expressions of so profound and philosophical a biologist may be regarded as the high-water mark of evolutionary thinking up to the date of the appearance of Wallace and Darwin's theory:—

'Even could the supporters of the development hypothesis merely show that the production of species by the process of modification is conceivable, they would be in a better position than their opponents. But they can do much more than this; they can show that the process of modification has effected and is effecting great changes in all organisms, subject to modifying influences ... they can show that any existing species—animal or vegetable—when placed under conditions different from its previous ones, immediately begins to undergo certain changes of structure fitting it for the new conditions. They can show that in successive generations these changes continue until ultimately the new conditions become the natural ones. They can show that in cultivated plants and domesticated animals, and in the several races of men, these changes have uniformly taken place. They can show that the degrees of difference, so produced, are often, as in dogs, greater than those on which distinctions of species are in other cases founded. They can show that it is a matter of dispute whether some of these modified forms *are* varieties or modified species. They can show too that the changes daily taking place in ourselves; the facility that attends long practice, and the loss of aptitude that begins when practice ceases; the development of every faculty, bodily, moral or intellectual, according to the use made of it, are all explicable on this same principle. And thus they can show that throughout all organic nature there *is* at work a modifying influence of the kind they assign as the cause of these specific differences, an influence which, though slow in its action, does in time, if the circumstances demand it, produce marked changes; an influence which, to all appearance, would produce in the millions of years, and under the great varieties of condition which geological records imply, any amount of change.'

This admirable passage, written seven years before the publication of the 'Origin of Species,' contains explicitly almost every idea that ordinary people, not specially biological in their interests, now associate with the name of Darwin. That is to say, it contains, in a very philosophical and abstract form, the theory of 'descent with modification' *without* the distinctive Darwinian adjunct of 'natural selection' or 'survival of the fittest.' Yet it was just that particular lever, dexterously applied, and carefully weighted with the whole weight of his endlessly accumulated inductive instances, that finally enabled our modern Archimedes in so short a time to move the world. The public, that was deaf to the high philosophy of Herbert Spencer, listened at once to the practical wisdom of Charles Darwin. They did not care at all for the *a priori* proof, but they believed forthwith as soon as a cautious and careful investigator laid bare before their eyes in minute detail the *modus operandi* of nature herself.

The main argument of Darwin's chief work runs somewhat after the following fashion[2]:—

Variation, to a greater or less degree, is a common and well-known fact in nature. More especially, animals and plants under domestication tend to vary from one another far more than do the individuals of any one species in the wild state. Rabbits in a warren are all alike in shape, size, colour, and features: rabbits in a hutch vary indefinitely in the hue of their fur, the length of their ears, the character of their coat, and half a dozen other minor particulars, well known to the observant souls of boys and fanciers. This great variability, though partly perhaps referable to excess of food, is probably due on the whole to their having been raised under conditions of life not so uniform as, and somewhat different from, those to which the parent species is commonly exposed in a state of nature. In other words, variability is one result of altered and more varied surrounding circumstances.

Again, this variability is usually indefinite. You cannot say what direction it will take, or to what particular results it is likely in any special instance to lead. Marked differences sometimes occur even between the young of the same litter, or between the seedlings sown from the same capsule. As a rule, the variations exhibit themselves in connection with sexual reproduction; but sometimes, as in the case of 'sporting plants,' a new bud suddenly produces leaves or flowers of a different character from the rest of those on the self-same stem, thus showing that the tendency to vary is inherent, as it were, in the organism itself. Upon this fundamental fact of the existence in nature of numerous and indefinite variations, the whole theory of natural selection is ultimately built up. In illustrating by example the immense variability of domesticated creatures, Darwin lays great stress upon the case of pigeons, with which he was familiar from his long experience as a breeder and fancier in his own home at Down. Naturalists are almost universally of opinion that all the breeds of domestic pigeons, from the carrier to the tumbler, from the runt to the fantail, are alike descended from the wild rock pigeon of the European coasts. The immense amount of variation which this original species has

[2] The remainder of the present chapter, which consists almost entirely of an exposition of the doctrine of natural selection, may safely be skipped by the reader already well acquainted with the Origin of Species. The abstract is taken for the most part from the latest and fullest enlarged edition, but attention is usually called in passing to the points which did not appear in the first issue of 1859.

undergone in domestication may be seen by comparing the numberless breeds of pigeon now exhibited at all our poultry shows with one another.

But variation gives us only half the elements of the ultimate problem, even in the case of domestic kinds. For the other half, we must have recourse to human selection, which, by picking out for seed or breeding purposes certain specially favoured varieties, has produced at last all the purposive or intentional diversity between the different existing stocks or breeds. In these artificially produced domestic races we see everywhere special adaptations to man's particular use or fancy. The dray-horse has been fashioned for purposes of strength and sure-footedness in draught, the race-horse for purposes of fleetness in running. In the fox-hound, man has encouraged the special properties that tend to produce a good day's hunting; in the sheepdog, those that make for the better maintenance and safety of a herd. The cauliflower is a cabbage, with specialised and somewhat abortive flower-heads; the fuller's teasel is a sport of the wild form, with curved hooks specially adapted by a freak of nature for the teasing of wool. So in every case man, by deliberately picking out for breeding or seeding purposes the accidental variations which happened best to suit his own needs, has succeeded at last in producing races admirably fitted in the minutest particulars for the special functions to which they are applied. There appears indeed to be hardly any limit to the almost infinite plasticity and modifiability of domestic animals. 'It would seem,' said a great sheep-breeder, speaking of sheep, 'as if farmers had chalked out upon a wall a form perfect in itself, and then proceeded to give it existence.'

Now, what is thus true within narrow limits, and in a short space of time about the deliberate action of man, Darwin showed to be also true within wider limits and spread over longer geological epochs about the unconscious action of nature. And herein consisted his great advance upon the earlier evolutionism of Lamarck, Goethe, and Erasmus Darwin. For while these instinctive pioneers of the evolutionary spirit saw clearly that animals and plants betrayed signs of common descent from one or a few original ancestors, they did not see what was the mechanism by which such organisms had been differentiated into so many distinct genera and species. They caught, indeed, at the analogy of variation under domestication and in the wild state, but they missed the subtler and deeper analogy between human and natural selection. Now, variation alone would give us a world consisting not of definite kinds fairly well demarcated one from the other, but of innumerable unclassified and unorganisable individuals, all shading off indefinitely one into the other, and incapable of being reduced by human ingenuity to any orderly hierarchical system. Furthermore, it would give us creatures without special adaptation of any kind to the peculiar circumstances of their own environment. To account for adaptation, for the almost perfect fitness of every plant and every animal to its position in life, for the existence (in other words) of definitely correlated parts and organs, we must call in the aid of survival of the fittest. Without that potent selective agent, our conception of the becoming of life is a mere chaos; order and organisation are utterly inexplicable save by the brilliant illuminating ray of the Darwinian principle. That is why Darwin destroyed at one blow the specious arguments of the early teleologists; he showed that where

Chambers and even Erasmus Darwin had seen the working of a final cause, we ought rather to recognise the working of an efficient cause, whose outcome necessarily but fallaciously simulates the supposed features of an *a priori* finality.

From art, then, Darwin harks back once more to nature. He proceeds to show that variability occurs among all wild plants and animals, though not so frequently under ordinary circumstances as in the case of domesticated species. Individual differences everywhere occur between plant and plant, between animal and animal. Sometimes these differences are so very numerous that it is impossible to divide the individuals at all into well-marked kinds; for example, among British wild-roses, brambles, hawkweeds and epilobes, with a few other very variable families, Babington makes as many as 251 distinct species, where Bentham gives only 112—a margin of 139 doubtful forms of shadowy indefiniteness. Varieties, in fact, are always arising, and dominant species in particular always tend to vary most in every direction. The reason why variation is not so marked in the wild state as under domestication is of course because the conditions are there less diverse; but where the conditions of wild things are most diverse, as in the case of dominant kinds, which range over a wide space of country or of ocean, abundant individual variations habitually occur. Local varieties thus produced are regarded by Darwin as incipient species: they are the raw material on which natural selection gradually exerts itself in the struggle for existence.

Granting individual variability, then, how do species arise in nature? And how are all the exquisite adaptations of part to whole, and of whole to environment, gradually initiated, improved, and perfected?

Here Malthus and the struggle for life come in to help us.

For the world is perpetually over-populated. It is not, as many good people fearfully imagine, on a half-comprehension of the Malthusian principle, shortly going to be over-populated; it is now, it has always been, and it will always be, pressed close up to the utmost possible limit of population. Reproduction is everywhere and in all species for ever outrunning means of subsistence; and starvation or competition is for ever keeping down the number of the offspring to the level of the average or normal supply of raw material. A single red campion produces in a year three thousand seeds; but there are not this year three thousand times as many red campions as there were last summer, nor will there be three thousand times as many more in the succeeding season. The roe of a cod contains sometimes nearly ten million eggs; but supposing each of these produced a young fish which arrived at maturity, the whole sea would immediately become a solid mass of closely packed codfish. Linnæus reckoned that if an annual plant had two seeds, each of which produced two seedlings in the succeeding season, and so on continually, in twenty years their progeny would amount to a million plants. A struggle for existence necessarily results from this universal tendency of animals and plants to increase faster than the means of subsistence, whether those means be food, as in the first case, or carbonic acid, water, and sunshine as in the second. Animals are all perpetually battling with one another for the food-supply of the moment; plants are perpetually battling with one another for their share of the soil, the rainfall, and the sunshine.

The case of the plant is a very important one to understand in this connection, because it is probable that most people greatly misunderstand the biological meaning of the phrase 'struggle for existence.' They imagine that the struggle is chiefly conducted between different species, whereas in reality it is chiefly conducted between members of the same species. It is not so much the battle between the tiger and the antelope, between the wolf and the bison, between the snake and the bird, that ultimately results in natural selection or survival of the fittest, as the struggle between tiger and tiger, between bison and bison, between snake and snake, between antelope and antelope. A human analogy may help to make this difficult principle a little clearer. The baker does not fear the competition of the butcher in the struggle for life: it is the competition of the other bakers that sometimes inexorably crushes him out of existence. The lawyer does not press hard upon the doctor, nor the architect upon the journeyman painter. A war in the Soudan or in South Africa is far less fatal to the workman in our great towns than the ceaseless competition of his fellow-workmen. It is not the soldier that kills the artisan, but the number of other artisans who undersell him and crowd to fill up every vacant position. In this way the great enemies of the individual herbivore are not the carnivores, but the other herbivores. The lion eats the antelope, to be sure; but the real struggle lies between lion and lion for a fair share of meat, or between antelope and antelope for a fair share of pasturage. *Homo homini lupus*, says the old proverb, and so, we may add, in a wider sense, *lupus lupo lupus*, also. Of course, the carnivore plays a great part in the selective process; but he is the selector only; the real competition is between the selected. Now, let us take the case of the plant. A thousand seedlings occupy the space where few alone can ultimately grow; and between these seedlings the struggle is fierce, the strongest and best adapted ultimately surviving. To take Darwin's own example, the mistletoe, which is a parasite, cannot truly be said to struggle with the apple tree on which it fastens; for if too many parasites cover a tree, it perishes, and so they kill themselves as well as their host, all alike dying together. But several seedling mistletoes growing together on the same branch may fairly be said to struggle with one another for light and air; and since mistletoe seeds are disseminated by birds and dropped by them in the angles of branches, the mistletoe may also be said to compete with other berry-bearing bushes, like cornel and hawthorn, for the ministrations of the fruit-eating birds. The struggle is fierce between allied kinds, and fiercest of all between individual members of the same species.

Owing to this constant struggle, variations, however slight, and from whatever cause arising, if in any degree profitable to the individual which presents them, will tend to the preservation of the particular organism, and, being on the average inherited by its offspring, will similarly tend to increase and multiply in the world at large. This is the principle of natural selection or survival of the fittest—the great principle which Darwin and Wallace added to the evolutionism of Lamarck and his successors.

Let us take a single concrete example. In the desert, with its monotonous sandy colouring, a black insect or a white insect, still more a red insect or a blue insect, would be immediately detected and promptly devoured by its natural enemies, the birds and lizards. But any greyish or yellowish insects would be less likely to attract attention at first sight, and would be overlooked as long as there were any more conspicuous individuals of their own kind about for the birds and lizards to feed on at their leisure. Hence, in a very short time, the desert would be depopulated of all but the greyest and yellowest insects; and among these the birds would pick out those which differed most markedly in hue or shade from the sand around them. But those which happened to vary most in the direction of a sandy or spotty colour would be most likely to survive, and to become the parents of future generations. Thus, in the course of long ages, all the insects which inhabit deserts have become sand-coloured; because the least sandy were perpetually picked out for destruction by their ever-watchful foes, while the most sandy escaped and multiplied and replenished the earth with their own likes.

Conversely, the birds and the lizards again would probably begin by being black, and white, and blue, and green, like most other birds and lizards in the world generally. But the insect would have ample warning of the near approach of such conspicuous self-advertising enemies, and would avoid them accordingly whenever they appeared within range of his limited vision, either by lying close, or by shamming death, or by retreating precipitately to holes and crannies. Therefore, whatever individual birds or lizards happened to vary most in the direction of grey or sand-colour, and so to creep unobserved upon the unguarded insects, would succeed best on the average in catching beetles or desert grasshoppers. Hence, by the slow dying out of the more highly coloured and distinctive insect-eaters, before the severe competition of the greyest and sandiest, all the birds and lizards of the desert have become at last as absolutely sand-coloured as the insects themselves. Only the greyest insect could escape the bird; only the greyest bird, *en revanche*, could surprise and devour the unwary insect.

Sir Charles Lyell and the elder De Candolle had already seen the great importance of the struggle for existence in the organic world, but neither of them had observed the magnificent corollary of natural selection, which flows from it almost as a mathematical necessity when once suggested; for, given indefinite variability, and a geometrical, rate of increase, it must needs follow that some varieties will be better suited to the circumstances than others, and therefore that they will survive on the average in increased proportions. A passage from one of Lyell's early letters will show how near he too went to this great luminous generalisation, and yet how utterly he missed the true implications of his own vague and chaotic idea. He writes thus to Sir John Herschel in 1836, while Darwin was still but homeward bound on the voyage of the 'Beagle':—

'In regard to the origination of new species, I am very glad to find that you think it probable that it may be carried on through the intervention of intermediate causes.... An insect may be made in one of its transformations to resemble a dead stick, or a leaf, or a lichen, or a stone, so as to be somewhat less easily found by its enemies; or if this would make it too strong, an occasional variety of the species may have this advantage conferred on it; or if this would be still too much, one sex of a certain variety. Probably there is scarcely a dash of colour on the wing or body of which the choice would be quite arbitrary, or which might not affect its duration for thousands of years.'

Now, this comes in some ways perilously near to Darwin indeed; but in the most important point of all it is wide apart from him as the pole is from the equator. For Lyell thought of all this as a matter of external teleological arrangement; he imagined a deliberate power from outside settling it all by design beforehand, and granting to varieties or species these special peculiarities in a manner that was at bottom essentially supernatural, or in other words miraculous; whereas Darwin thinks of it as the necessary result of the circumstances themselves, an inevitable outcome of indefinite variability *plus* the geometrical rate of increase. Where Lyell sees a final cause, Darwin sees an efficient cause; and this distinction is fundamental. It marks Darwin's position as that of a great philosophical thinker, who can dash aside at once all metaphysical cobwebs, and penetrate to the inmost recesses of things, unswerved by the vain but specious allurements of obvious and misleading teleological fallacies.

Darwin also laid great stress on the immense complexity of the relations which animals and plants bear to one another, in the struggle for existence. For example, on the heathy uplands near Farnham in Surrey, large spaces were at one time enclosed, on which, within ten years, self-grown fir-trees from the wind-borne seeds of distant clumps sprang up so thickly as actually to choke one another with their tiny branches. All over the heaths outside, when Darwin looked for them, he could not find a single fir, except the old clumps on the hilltops, from which the seedlings themselves had originally sprung. But, on looking closer among the stems of the heath, he descried a number of very tiny firs, which had been perpetually browsed down by the cattle on the commons; and one of them, with twenty-six rings of growth, had during many years endeavoured unsuccessfully to raise its head above the surrounding heather. Hence, as soon as the land was enclosed, and the cattle excluded, it became covered at once with a thick growth of vigorous young fir-trees. Yet who would ever have supposed beforehand that the mere presence or absence of cattle would absolutely have determined the very existence of the Scotch fir throughout a wide range of well-adapted sandy English upland?

To take another curious instance mentioned by Darwin. In Paraguay, unlike the greater part of neighbouring South America, neither horses nor cattle have ever run wild. This is due to the presence of a parasitic fly, which lays its eggs in their bodies when first born, the maggots killing off the tender young in their first stages. But if any cause were to alter the number of the dangerous flies, then cattle and wild horses would abound; and this would alter the vegetation, as Darwin himself observed in other parts of America; and the change in the vegetation would affect the insects; and that again the insectivorous birds; and so on in ever widening circles of incalculable complexity. Once more, to quote the most famous instance of all, the visits of humble-bees are absolutely necessary in order to place the pollen in the right position for setting the seeds of purple clover. Heads from which Darwin excluded the bees produced no seeds at all. Hence, if humble-bees became extinct in England, the red clover, too, would die off: and indeed, in New Zealand, where there are no humble-bees, and where the efforts to introduce them for this very purpose have been uniformly unsuccessful, the clover never sets its seed at all, and fresh stocks have to be imported at great expense every year from Europe. But the number of humble-bees in any district largely depends upon the number of field-mice, which destroy the combs and nests in immense quantities. The number of mice, again, is greatly affected by the proportion of cats in the neighbourhood; so that Colonel Newman, who paid much attention to this subject, found humble-bees most numerous in the neighbourhood of villages and small towns, an effect which he attributed to the abundance of cats, and the consequent scarcity of the destructive field-mice. Yet here once more, who could suppose beforehand that the degree to which the purple clover set its seeds was in part determined by the number of cats kept in houses in the surrounding district?

One of Darwin's own favourite examples of the action of natural selection, which he afterwards expanded largely in his work on Orchids and in several other volumes, is that which relates to the origin of conspicuous flowers. Many plants have a sweet excretion, which is eliminated sometimes even by the leaves, as in the case of the common laurel. This juice, though small in quantity, is eagerly sought and eaten by insects. Now let us suppose that, in some variety of an inconspicuous flower, similar nectar was produced in the neighbourhood of the petals and stamens. Insects, in seeking the nectar, would dust their bodies over with the pollen, and would carry it away with them to the next flower visited. This would result in an act of crossing; and that act, as Darwin afterwards abundantly proved in a separate and very laborious treatise, gives rise to exceptionally vigorous seedlings, which would therefore have the best chance of flourishing and surviving in the struggle for existence. The flowers which produced most honey would oftenest be visited, and oftenest crossed; so that they would finally form a new species. The more brightly coloured among them, again, would be more readily discriminated than the less brightly coloured; and this would give them such an advantage that in the long run, as we actually see, almost all habitually insect-fertilised flowers would come to have brilliant petals. The germ of this luminous idea, once more, is to be found in Sprengel's remarkable work on the fertilisation of flowers—a work far in advance of its time in many ways, and to which Darwin always expressed his deep obligations; but, as in so many other instances, while Sprengel looked upon all the little modifications and adaptations of flower and insect to one another as the result of distinct creative design, Darwin looked upon them as the result of natural selection, working upon the basis of indeterminate spontaneous variations.

How do these variations arise? Not by chance, of course (for in the strict scientific sense nothing on earth can be considered as really fortuitous), but as the outcome for the most part of very minute organic causes, whose particular action it is impossible for us to predict with our present knowledge. Some physical cause in each case there must necessarily be; and indeed it is often possible to show that certain changes of condition in the parent do result in variations in the offspring, though what special direction the variation will take can never be foretold with any accuracy. In short, our ignorance of the laws of variation is profound, but our knowledge of the fact is clear and certain. The fact alone is essential to the principle of natural selection; the cause, though in itself an interesting subject of inquiry, may be safely laid aside for the present as comparatively unimportant. What we have actually given to us in the concrete universe is, organisms varying perpetually in minute points, and a rapid rate of increase causing every minute point of advantage to be exceptionally favoured in the struggle for existence.

But Darwin is remarkable among all broachers of new theories for the extraordinary candour and openness of his method. He acknowledged beforehand all the difficulties in the way of his theory, and though he himself confessed that some of them were serious (a statement which subsequent research has often rendered unnecessary), he met many of them with cogent arguments by anticipation, and demolished objections before they could even be raised against him by hostile critics. Of these objections, only two need here be mentioned. The first is the question, why is not all nature even now a confused mass of transitional forms? Why do genera and species exist as we see them at present in broad distinction one from the other? To this Darwin answers rightly that, where the process of species-making is still going on, we do actually find fine gradations and transitional forms existing between genera, varieties, and species.[3] But, furthermore, as natural selection acts solely by the preservation of useful modifications, each better-adapted new form will always tend in a fully stocked country to oust and exterminate its own unimproved parent type, as well as all other competing but less perfect varieties. Thus natural selection and extinction of intermediates go for ever hand in hand. The more perfect the new variety, the more absolutely will it kill off the intermediate forms. The second great difficulty lies in the question of the origin of instinct, which, as Darwin shows, by careful inductive instances, may have arisen by the slow and gradual accumulation of numerous slight yet profitable variations.

I have dwelt at some length upon those portions of the 'Origin of Species' which deal in detail with the theory of natural selection, the chief contribution which Darwin made to the evolutionary movement, because it is impossible otherwise fully to understand the great gulf which separates his evolutionism from the earlier evolutionism of Lamarck and his followers. But it is impracticable here to give any idea of the immense wealth of example and illustration which Darwin brought to the elucidation of every part of his complex problem. In order to gain a full conception of this side of his nature, we must turn to the original treatise itself, and still more to the subsequent volumes in which the ground-work of observations and experiments on which he based his theory was more fully detailed for the specialist public.

The remainder of Darwin's epoch-making work deals, strictly speaking, rather with the general theory of 'descent with modification' than with the special doctrine of natural selection. It restates and reinforces, by the light of the new additional concept, and with fuller facts and later knowledge, the four great arguments already known in favour of organic evolution as a whole, the argument from Geological Succession, the argument from Geographical Distribution, the ar-

[3] The researches of Seebohm and others have since proved that this is really the case to a far greater extent than Darwin was aware of in 1859, or, indeed, till many years afterward.

gument from Embryological Development, and the argument from Classificatory Affinities. Each of these we may briefly summarise.

The geological record is confessedly imperfect. At the time when Darwin first published the 'Origin of Species,' it had disclosed to our view comparatively few intermediate or transitional forms between the chief great classes of plants or animals; since that time, in singular confirmation of the Darwinian hypothesis, it has disclosed an immense number of such connecting types, amongst which may be more particularly noticed the 'missing links' between the birds and reptiles, the ancestors of the horses, the camels, and the pigs, and the common progenitor of the ruminants and the pachyderms, two great groups classed by Cuvier as distinct orders—all of which instances were incorporated by Darwin in later editions of his 'Origin of Species.' But, apart from these special and newly discovered cases, the whole general course of geological history 'agrees admirably with the theory of descent with modification through variation and natural selection.' The simpler animals of early times are followed by the more complex and more specialised animals of later geological periods. As each main group of animals appears upon the stage of life, it appears in a very central and 'generalised' form; as time goes on, we find its various members differing more and more widely from one another, and assuming more and more specialised adaptive forms. And in each country it is found, as a rule, that the extinct animals of the later formations bear a close general resemblance and relationship to the animals which now inhabit the same regions. For example, the fossil mammals from the Australian caves are nearly allied to the modern kangaroos, phalangers, and wombats; and the gigantic extinct sloths and armadillos of South America are reproduced in their smaller representatives at the present day. So, too, the moa of New Zealand was a huge apteryx; and the birds disentombed from the bone-caves of Brazil show close affinities to the toucans and jacanars that still scream and flit in countless flocks among Brazilian forests. The obvious implication is that the animals now inhabiting any given area are the modified descendants of those that formerly inhabited it. 'On the theory of descent with modification, the great law of the succession of the same types within the same areas is at once explained.'

This last consideration leads us up to the argument from Geographical Distribution. In considering the various local faunas and floras on the face of the globe, no point strikes one more forcibly than the fact that neither their similarities nor their dissimilarities can be accounted for by climate or physical conditions. The animals of South Africa do not in the least resemble the animals of the corresponding belt of South America; the Australian beasts and birds and trees are utterly unlike those of France and Germany; the fishes and crustaceans of the Pacific at Panama are widely different from those of the Caribbean at the same point, separated from them only by the narrow belt of intervening isthmus. On the other hand, within the same continuous areas of sea or land, however great the differences of physical conditions, we find everywhere closely related types in possession of the most distinct and varied situations. On the burning plains of La Plata we get the agouti and the bizcacha as the chief rodents; we ascend the Cordillera, and close to the eternal snows we discover, not hares and rabbits like those of Europe, but a specialised chilly mountain form of the same distinctly South American type. We turn to the rivers, and we see no musk-rat or beaver, but the coypu and capybara, slightly altered varieties of the original bizcacha ancestor. Australia has no wolf, but it has instead fierce and active carnivorous marsupials; it has no mice, but some of its tiny kangaroo-like creatures fulfil analogous functions in its animal economy. Everywhere the evidence points to the conclusion that local species have been locally evolved from pre-existing similar species. The oceanic isles, of which Darwin had had so large an experience, and especially his old friends the Galapagos, come in usefully for this stage of the question. They are invariably inhabited, as Darwin pointed out, and as Wallace has since abundantly shown in the minutest detail, by waifs and strays from neighbouring continents, altered and specialised by natural selection in accordance with the conditions of their new habitat. As a rule, they point back to the districts whence blow the strongest and most prevalent winds; and the modifications they have undergone are largely dependent upon the nature of the other species with which they have to compete, or to whose habits they must needs accommodate themselves. In such cases it is easy to see how far Darwin's special conception of natural selection helps to explain and account for facts not easily explicable by the older evolutionism of mere descent with modification.

Embryology, the study of early development in the individual animal or plant, also throws much side light upon the nature and ancestry of each species or family. For example, gorse, which is a member of the pea-flower tribe, has in its adult stage solid, spiny, thorn-like leaves, none of which in the least resemble the foliage of the clover, to which it is closely related; but the young seedling in its earliest stages has trefoil leaves, which only slowly pass by infinitesimal gradations into flat blades and finally into the familiar defensive prickles. Here, natural selection under stress of herbivorous animals on open heaths and commons has spared only those particular gorse-bushes which varied in the direction of the stiffest and most inedible foliage; but the young plant in its first days still preserves for us the trefoil leaf which it shared originally with a vast group of clover-like congeners. The adult barnacle, once more, presents a certain fallacious external resemblance to a mollusk, and was actually so classed even by the penetrating and systematic intellect of Cuvier; but a glance at the larva shows an instructed eye at once that it is really a shell-making and abnormal crustacean. On a wider scale, the embryos of mammals are at first indistinguishable from those of birds or reptiles; the feet of lizards, the hoofs of horses, the hands of man, the wings of the bat, the pinions of birds, all arise from the same fundamental shapeless bud, in the same spot of an almost identical embryo. Even the human foetus, at a certain stage of its development, is provided with gill-slits, which point dimly back to the remote ages when its ancestor was something very like a fish. The embryo is a picture, more or less obscured and blurred in its outline, of the common progenitor of a whole great class of plants or animals.

Finally, classification points in the same way to the affiliation of all existing genera and species upon certain early divergent ancestors. The whole scheme of the biological system, as initiated by Linnæus and improved by Cuvier, Jussieu, De Candolle, and their successors, is essentially that of a genealogical tree. The prime central vertebrate ancestor—to take the case of the creatures most familiar to the general reader—appears to have been an animal not unlike the existing lancelet, a mud-haunting, cartilaginous, undeveloped fish, whose main lineaments are also embryologically preserved for us in the ascidian larva and the common tadpole. From this early common centre have been developed, apparently, in one direction the fishes, and in another the amphibian tribes of frogs, newts, salamanders, and axolotls. From an early amphibian, again, the common ancestor of birds, reptiles, and mammals seems to have diverged: the intermediate links between bird and reptile being faintly traced among the extinct deinosaurians and the archæopteryx, some years subsequently to the first appearance of the 'Origin of Species;' while the ornithorhyncus, which to some extent connects the mammals, and especially the marsupials, with the lower egg-laying types of vertebrate, was already well-known and thoroughly studied before the publication of Darwin's great work. Throughout, the indications given by all the chief tribes of animals and plants point back to slow descent and divergence from common ancestors; and all the subsequent course of palæontological research has supplied us rapidly, one after another, with the remains of just such undifferentiated family starting-points.

Stress has mainly been laid, in this brief and necessarily imperfect abstract, on the essentially Darwinian principle of natural selection. But Darwin did not himself attribute everything to this potent factor in the moulding of species. 'I am convinced,' he wrote pointedly in the introduction to his first edition, 'that natural selection has been the main but not the exclusive means of modification.' He attributed considerable importance as well to the Lamarckian principle of use and disuse, already so fully insisted upon before him by Mr. Herbert Spencer. The chief factors in his compound theory, as given in his own words at the end of his work, areas follows: 'Growth with Reproduction; Inheritance, which is almost implied by reproduction; Variability, from the indirect and direct action of the conditions of life, and from use and disuse; a Ratio of Increase, so high as to lead to a Struggle for Life, and as a consequence to Natural Selection, entailing Divergence of Character, and the Extinction of the less improved forms. Thus, from the war of nature, from famine and death, the most exalted object which we are capable of conceiving, namely, the production of the higher animals, directly follows.'

Such was the simple and inoffensive-looking bombshell which Darwin launched from his quiet home at Down into the very midst of the teleological camp in the peaceful year 1859. Subsequent generations will remember the date as a crisis and turning-point in the history of mankind.

# CHAPTER VII.

## THE DARWINIAN REVOLUTION BEGINS.

So far as the scientific world was concerned the 'Origin of Species' fell, like a grain of mustard seed, upon good and well-prepared ground; the plant that sprang from it grew up forthwith into a great and stately tree, that overshadowed with its spreading branches all the corners of the earth.

The soil, indeed, had been carefully broken for it beforehand: Lamarck and St. Hilaire, Spencer and Chambers, had ploughed and harrowed in all diligence; and the minds of men were thoroughly ready for the assimilation of the new doctrine. But the seed itself, too, was the right germ for the exact moment; it contained within itself the vivifying principle that enabled it to grow and wax exceeding great where kindred germs before had withered away, or had borne but scanty and immature fruit.

Two conditions contributed to this result, one external, the other internal.

First for the less important external consideration. Darwin himself was a sound man with an established reputation for solidity and learning. That gained for his theory from the very first outset universal respect and a fair hearing. Herbert Spencer was known to be a philosopher: and the practical English nation mistrusts philosophers: those people probe too deep and soar too high for any sensible person to follow them in all their flights. Robert Chambers, the unknown author of 'Vestiges of Creation,' was a shallow sciolist; it was whispered abroad that he was even inaccurate and slovenly in his facts: and your scientific plodder detests the very shadow of minute inaccuracy, though it speak with the tongues of men and angels, and be bound up with all the grasp and power of a Newton or a Goethe. But Charles Darwin was a known personage, an F.R.S., a distinguished authority upon coral reefs and barnacles, a great geologist, a great biologist, a great observer and indefatigable collector. His book came into the public hands stamped with the imprimatur of official recognition. Darwin was the father of the infant theory; Lyell and Hooker stood for its sponsors. The world could not afford to despise its contents; they could not brand its author offhand as a clever dreamer or a foolish amateur, or consign him to the dreaded English limbo of the 'mere theorist.'

Next, for the other and far more important internal consideration. The book itself was one of the greatest, the most learned, the most lucid, the most logical, the most crushing, the most conclusive, that the world had ever yet seen. Step by step, and principle by principle, it proved every point in its progress triumphantly before it went on to demonstrate the next. So vast an array of facts so thoroughly in hand had never before been mustered and marshalled in favour of any biological theory. Those who had insight to learn and understand were convinced at once by the cogency of the argument; those who had not were overpowered and silenced by the weight of the authority and the mass of the learning. A hot battle burst forth at once, no doubt, around the successful volume; but it was one of those battles which are aroused only by great truths,—a battle in which the victory is a foregone conclusion, and the rancour of the assailants the highest compliment to the prowess of the assailed.

Darwin himself, in his quiet country home at Down, was simply astonished at the rapid success of his own work. The first edition was published at the end of November 1859; it was exhausted almost immediately, and a second was got ready in hot haste by the beginning of January 1860. In less than six weeks the book had become famous, and Darwin found himself the centre of a European contest, waged with exceeding bitterness, over the truth or falsity of his wonderful volume. To the world at large Darwinism and evolution became at once synonymous terms. The same people who would entirely ascribe the Protestant Reformation to the account of Luther, and the inductive philosophy to the account of Bacon, also believed, in the simplicity of their hearts, that the whole vast evolutionary movement was due at bottom to that very insidious and dangerous book of Mr. Darwin's.

The fact is, profound as had been the impulses in the evolutionary direction among men of science before Darwin's work appeared at all, immense as were the throes and pangs of labour throughout all Europe which preceded and accompanied its actual birth, when it came at last it came to the general world of unscientific readers with all the sudden vividness and novelty of a tremendous earthquake. Long predestined, it was yet wholly unexpected. Men at large had known nothing or next to nothing of this colossal but hidden revolutionary force which had been gathering head and energy for so many years unseen within the bowels of the earth; and now that its outer manifestation had actually burst upon them, they felt the solid ground of dogmatic security bodily giving way beneath their feet, and knew not where to turn in their extremity for support. Naturally, it was the theological interest that felt itself at first most forcibly assailed. The first few chapters of Genesis, or rather the belief in their scientific and historical character, already sapped by the revelations of geology, seemed to orthodox defenders to be fatally undermined if the Darwinian hypothesis were once to meet with general recognition. The first resource of menaced orthodoxy is always to deny the alleged facts; the second is to patch up tardily the feeble and hollow *modus vivendi* of an artificial pact. On this occasion the orthodox acted strictly after their kind: but to their credit it should be added that they yielded gracefully in the long run to the unanimous voice of scientific opinion. Twenty-three years later, when all that was mortal of Charles Darwin was being borne with pomp and pageantry to its last resting-place in Westminster Abbey, enlightened orthodoxy, with generous oblivion, ratified a truce over the dead body of the great leader, and, outgrowing its original dread of naturalistic interpretations, accepted his theory without reserve as 'not necessarily hostile to the main fundamental truths of religion.' Let us render justice to the vanquished in a memorable struggle. Churchmen followed respectfully to the grave with frank and noble inconsistency the honoured remains of the very teacher whom less than a quarter of a century earlier they had naturally dreaded as loosening the traditional foundations of all accepted religion and morality.

But if the attack was fierce and bitter, the defence was assisted by a sudden access of powerful forces from friendly quarters. A few of the elder generation of naturalists held out, indeed, for various shorter or longer periods; some of them never came into the camp at all, but lingered on, left behind, like stragglers from the onward march, by the younger biologists, in isolated non-conformity on the lonely heights of austere officialism. Their business was to ticket and docket and pigeon-hole, not to venture abroad on untried wings into the airy regions of philosophical speculation. The elder men, in fact, had many of them lost that elasticity and modifiability of intellect which is necessary for the reception of new and revolutionary fundamental concepts. A mind that has hardened down into the last stage of extreme maturity may assimilate fresh facts and fresh minor principles, but it cannot assimilate fresh synthetic systems of the entire cosmos. Moreover, some of the elder thinkers were committed beforehand to opposing views, with which they lacked either the courage or the intellectual power to break; while others were entangled by religious restrictions, and unable to free themselves from the cramping fetters of a narrow orthodoxy. But even among his own contemporaries and seniors Darwin found not a few whose minds were thoroughly prepared beforehand for the reception of his lucid and luminous hypothesis; while the younger naturalists, with the plasticity of youth, assimilated almost to a man, with the utmost avidity, the great truths thus showered down upon them by the preacher of evolution.

Sir Joseph Hooker and Professor Huxley were among the first to give in their adhesion and stand up boldly for the new truth by the side of the reckless and disturbing innovator. In June 1859, nearly a year after the reading of the Darwin-Wallace papers at the Linnean Society, but five months previously to the publication of the 'Origin of Species,' Huxley lectured at the Royal Institution on 'Persistent Types of Animal Life,' and declared against the old barren theory of successive creations, in favour of the new and fruitful hypothesis of gradual modification. In December 1859, a month later than the appearance of Darwin's book, Hooker published his 'Introduction to the Flora of Australia,' in the first part of which he championed the belief in the descent and modification of species, and enforced his views by many original observations drawn from the domain of botanical science. For fifteen years, as Darwin himself gratefully observed in his introduction to the 'Origin of Species,' that learned botanist had shared the secret of natural selection, and aided its author in every possible way by his large stores of knowledge and his excellent judgment. Bates, the naturalist on the Amazons, followed fast with his beautiful and striking theory of mimicry, a crucial instance well explained. The facts of the strange disguises which birds and insects often assume had long been present to his acute mind, and he hailed with delight the discovery of the new principle, which at once enabled him to reduce them with ease to symmetry and order. To Herbert Spencer, an evolutionist in fibre from the very beginning, the fresh doctrine of natural selection came like a powerful ally and an unexpected assistant in deciphering the deep fundamental problems on which he was at that moment actually engaged; and in his 'Principles of Biology,' even then in contemplation, he at once adopted and utilised the new truth with all the keen and vigorous insight of his profound analytic and synthetic intellect. The first part of that important work was issued to subscribers just three years after the original appearance of the 'Origin of Species;' the first volume was fully completed in October 1864. It is to Mr. Spencer that we owe the pellucid expression 'survival of the fittest,' which conveys even better than Darwin's own phrase, 'natural selection,' the essential element added by the 'Origin of Species' to the pre-existing evolutionary conception.

The British Association for the Advancement of Science held its big annual doctrinaire picnic the next summer after the publication of Darwin's book, at Oxford. The Oxford meeting was a stormy and a well-remembered one. The 'Origin of Species' was there discussed and attacked before a biological section strangely enough presided over by Darwin's old Cambridge teacher, Professor Henslow. Though then a beneficed parish priest, Henslow had the boldness frankly to avow his own acceptance of his great pupil's startling conclusions. Huxley followed in the same path, as did also Lubbock and Hooker. On the whole, the evolutionists were already in the ascendant; the fresh young intellects especially being quick to seize upon the new pabulum so generously dealt out to them by the new evolutionism.

Among scientific minds of the first order, Lyell alone in England, heavily weighted by theological preconceptions, for awhile hung back. All his life long, as his letters show us, the great geologist had felt the powerful spell of the Lamarckian hypothesis continually enticing him with its seductive charm. He had fought against it blindly, in the passionate endeavour to preserve what he thought his higher faith in the separate and divine creation of man; but ever and anon he returned anew to the biological Circe with a fresh fascination, as the moth returns to the beautiful flame that has scorched and singed it. In a well-known passage in the earlier editions of his 'Principles of Geology,' the father of uniformitarianism gives at length his own reasons for dissenting from the doctrine of evolution as then set forth; and even after Darwin's discovery had supplied him with a new clue, a *vera causa*, a sufficient power for the modification of species into fresh forms, theological difficulties made him cling still as long as possible to the old theory of the origin of man which he loved to describe as that of the 'archangel ruined.' He was loth to exchange this cherished belief for the degrading alternative (as it approved itself to him) of the ape elevated. But in the end, with the fearless honesty of a searcher after truth, he gave way slowly and regretfully. Always looking back with something like remorse to the flesh-pots of the ecclesiastical Egypt, with its enticing visions of fallen grandeur, the great thinker whose uniformitarian theory of geology had more than aught else paved the way for the gradual acceptance of Darwin's evolutionism, came out at last from the house of bondage, and nobly ranged himself on the side of what his intellect judged to be the truth of nature, though his emotions urged him hard to blind his judgment and to neglect its lights for an emotional figment. Science has no more pathetic figure than that of the old philosopher, in his sixty-sixth year, throwing himself with all the eagerness of youth into what he had long considered the wrong scale, and vigorously wrecking in the 'Antiquity of Man' what seemed to the dimmed vision of his own emotional nature the very foundations of his beloved creed. But still he did it. He came out and was separate. In his own idiomatic language, he found at last that 'we must go the whole ourang;' and, deep as was the pang that the recantation cost him, he formally retracted the condemnation of 'transformism' in his earlier works, and accepted, however unwillingly, the theory he had so often and so deliberately rejected.

The 'Antiquity of Man' came out in February 1863, some three years after the 'Origin of Species.' For some time speculation had been active over the strange hatchets which Boucher de Perthes had recently unearthed among the Abbeville drift—shapeless masses of chipped flint rudely fashioned into the form of an axe, which we now call palæolithic implements, and know to be the handicraft of preglacial men. But until Lyell's authoritative work appeared the unscientific public could not tell exactly what to think of these curious and almost unhuman-looking objects. Lyell at once set all doubts at rest; the magic of his name silenced the derisive whispers of the dissidents. Already, in the previous year, the first fasciculus of Colenso's famous work on the Pentateuch had dealt a serious blow from the ecclesiastical and critical side at the authenticity and historical truth of the Mosaic cosmogony. Lyell now from the scientific side completely demolished its literal truth, as ordinarily interpreted, by throwing back the primitive origin of our race into a dim past of immeasurable antiquity. In so doing he was clearing the way for Charles Darwin's second great work, 'The Descent of Man;' and by incorporating in his book Huxley's remarks on the Neanderthal skull, and much similar evolutionary matter, he advertised the new creed in the animal origin of our race with all the acquired weight of his immense and justly-deserved European reputation. As a matter of taste, Lyell did not relish the application of evolutionism to his own species. But, with that perfect loyalty to fact which he shared so completely with Charles Darwin, as soon as he found the evidence overwhelming, he gave in. By that grudging concession he immensely strengthened the position of the new creed. 'I plead guilty,' he writes to Sir Joseph Hooker, 'to going farther in my reasoning towards transmutation than in my sentiments and imagination, and perhaps for that very reason I shall lead more people on to Darwin and you, than one who, being born later, like Lubbock, has comparatively little to abandon of old and long-cherished ideas, which constituted the charm to me of the theoretical part of the science in my earlier days.' And to Darwin himself he writes regretfully. 'The descent of man from the brutes takes away much of the charm from my speculations on the past relating to such matters.' This very reluctance itself told powerfully in favour of Charles Darwin's novel theories: there is no evidence more valuable to a cause than that which it extorts by moral force, in spite of himself, from the faltering lips of an unwilling witness.

The same year that saw the publication of Lyell's 'Antiquity of Man' saw also the first appearance of Huxley's work on 'Man's Place in Nature.' Darwin himself had been anxious rather than otherwise to avoid too close reference to the implications of his theory as regards the origin and destiny of the human race. He had desired that his strictly scientific views on the rise of specific distinctions should be judged entirely on their own merits, unhampered by the interference of real or supposed theological and ethical considerations. His own language on all such subjects, wherever he was compelled to trench on them in the 'Origin of Species,' was guarded and conciliatory; he scarcely referred at all to man or his history; and his occasional notices of the moving principle and first cause of the entire cosmos were reverential and religious in the truest sense and in the highest degree. But you cannot let loose a moral whirlwind, and then attempt to direct its course; you cannot open the floodgates of opinion or of speculation, and then pretend to set limits to the scope of their restless motion. Darwin soon found out that people would insist in drawing inferences beyond what was written, and in seeing implicit conclusions when they were not definitely formulated in the words of their author. 'Man is perennially interesting to man,' says the great chaotic American thinker; and whatever all-embracing truth you set before him, you may be sure that man will see in it chiefly the implications that most closely affect his own happiness and his own destiny. The biological question of the origin of species is a sufficiently wide one, but it includes also, among other cases, the origin of the very familiar species *Homo sapiens* of Linnæus. Some theologians jumped at once at the conclusion, right or wrong, that if Darwinism were true man was nothing more than a developed monkey, the immortal soul was an exploded myth, the foundations of religion itself were shattered, and the wave of infidelity was doomed to swamp the whole of Christendom with its blank nihilism. Scientific men, on the other hand, drew the conclusion that man must be descended, like other mammals, from some common early vertebrate ancestor, and that the current views of his origin and destiny must be largely modified by the evolutionary creed. Of this profound scientific belief Professor Huxley's maiden work was the earliest outcome.

Meantime, on the continent of Europe and over-sea in America, the Darwinian theory was being hotly debated and warmly defended. France, coldly sceptical and critical, positive rather than imaginative in matters of science, and little prone by native cast of mind to the evolutionary attitude, stood aloof to a great extent from the onward course of the general movement. Here and there, to be sure, a Gaudry or a Ribot, a Delboeuf or a De Candolle (the two latter a Liège Belgian and a Genevan Swiss) might heartily throw himself into the new ideas, and contribute whole squadrons of geological or botanical fact to the final victory. Yet, as a whole, the dry and cautious French intelligence, ever inclined to a scientific opportunism, preferred for the moment to stand by expectant and await the result of the European consensus. But philosophical Germany, on the other hand, beaming enthusiasm from its myriad spectacles, eagerly welcomed the novel ideas, and proclaimed from the housetops the evolutionary faith as a main plank in the rising platform of the newly-roused Kulturkampf. Fritz Müller began with all the ardour of a fresh convert to collect his admirable 'Facts for Darwin;' his brother Hermann sat down with indomitable patience, like the master's own, to watch the ceaseless action of the bees and butterflies in the fertilisation of flowers. Rütimeyer applied the Darwinian principles to the explanation of mammalian relationships, and Haeckel set to work upon his vast reconstructive 'History of Creation,' a largely speculative work which, with all its faults, distinctly carried forward the evolutionary impulse, and set fresh researchers working upon new lines, to confirm or to disprove its audacious imaginings. In America, Asa Gray gave to the young creed the high authority of his well-known name, and Chauncey Wright helped it onward on the road with all the restrained force of his singular and oblique but powerful and original personality. If Agassiz and Dawson still hesitated, Fiske and Youmans were ardent in the faith. If critical Boston put up its eye-glass doubtfully, Chicago and St. Louis were ready for conversion. Everywhere Darwin and Darwinism became as household words; it was the singular fate of the great prophet of evolution, alone almost among the sons of men, to hear his own name familiarly twisted during his own lifetime into a colloquial adjective, and to see the Darwinian theory and the errors of Darwinism staring him in the face a hundred times a day from every newspaper and every periodical.

Of course the 'Origin of Species' was largely translated at once into all the civilised languages of Europe, Russian as well as French, Dutch as well as German, Swedish as well as Italian, Spanish as well as Hungarian, nay even, at last, transcending narrow continental limits, Japanese as well as Hindustani. The revolution which it was rapidly effecting was indeed a revolution in every mode of thought and feeling as well as a revolution in mere restricted biological opinion. But all this time, the modest, single-minded, and unassuming author was working unmoved among his plants and pigeons in his home at Down, regardless of the European fame he was so quickly acquiring, and anxious only to bring to a termination the vast work which he still contemplated. A little more than eleven years intervened between the publication of the 'Origin of Species,' in 1859, and the first appearance of the 'Descent of Man,' in 1871. The interval was occupied in carrying out in part the gigantic scheme of his original collections for the full treatment of the development theory. The work published in 1859 Darwin regarded merely as an abstract and preliminary outline of his full opinions: 'No one can feel more sensible than I do,' he wrote, 'of the necessity of hereafter publishing in detail all the facts, with references, on which my conclusions have been grounded.' The marvellously learned work on the 'Variation of Animals and Plants under Domestication,' which came out in two volumes in 1867, formed the first instalment of this long-projected treatise. The second part, as he told Mr. Fiske, was to have treated of the variation of animals and plants through natural selection; while the third part would have dealt at length with the phenomena of morphology, of classification, and of distribution in space and time. But these latter portions of the work were never written. To say the truth, they were never needed. So universal was the recognition among the younger men of Darwin's discovery, that before ten years were over innumerable workers were pushing out the consequences of natural selection into every field of biology and palæontology. It seemed no longer so necessary as it had once seemed to write the larger and more elaborate treatise he had originally contemplated.

The volume on the variation of animals and plants contained also Darwin's one solitary contribution to the pure speculative philosophy of life—his 'Provisional Hypothesis of Pangenesis,' by which he strove to account on philosophical principles for the general facts of physical and mental heredity. Not to mince matters, it was his one conspicuous failure, and is now pretty universally admitted as such. Let not the love of the biographer deceive us; Darwin was here attempting a task *ultra vires*. As already observed, his mind, vast as it was, leaned rather to the concrete than to the abstract side: he lacked the distinctively metaphysical and speculative twist. Strange to say, too, his abortive theory appeared some years later than Herbert Spencer's magnificent all-sided conception of 'Physiological Units,' put forth expressly to meet the self-same difficulty. But while Darwin's hypothesis is rudely materialistic, Herbert Spencer's is built up by an acute and subtle analytical perception of all the analogous facts in universal nature. It is a singular instance of a crude and essentially unphilosophic conception endeavouring to replace a finished and delicate philosophical idea.

Earlier still, in 1862, Darwin had published his wonderful and fascinating book on the 'Fertilisation of Orchids.' It is delightful to contemplate the picture of the unruffled naturalist, in the midst of that universal storm of ecclesiastical obloquy and scientific enthusiasm which he had roused throughout Europe, sitting down calmly in his Kentish conservatory to watch the behaviour of catasetums and masdevallias, and to work out the details of his chosen subject, with that marvellous patience of which he was so great a master, in the pettiest minutiæ of fertilisation as displayed by a single highly developed family of plants. Whoever wishes to learn the full profundity of Darwin's researches, into every point that he set himself to investigate, cannot do better than turn for a while to the consideration of that exquisite treatise on one of the quaintest fairylands of science. He will there learn by what an extraordinary wealth of cunning devices natural selection has ensured the due conveyance of the fecundating pollen from stamens to stigmas within the limits of a single group of vegetable organisms. Here the fertilising mass is gummed automatically between the eyes of the exploring bee, and then bent round by the drying of its stalk so as to come in contact with the stigmatic surface. There the pollen club is jerked out elastically by a sensitive fibre, and actually flung by its irritable antennæ at the unconscious head of the fertilising insect. In one case, the lip of the flower secretes moisture and forms a sort of cold bath, which wets the wings of the bees, so compelling them to creep out of the bucket by a passage close to the anthers and stigma; in another case, the honey is concealed at the bottom of so long a tube that only the proper fertilising moth with a proboscis of ten or eleven inches in length can probe the deep recess in which it is hidden. These, and a hundred other similar instances, were all carefully considered and described by the great naturalist as the by-work with which he filled up one of the intervals between his greater and more comprehensive treatises.

In the decade between 1860 and 1870 the progress of Darwinism was rapid and continuous. One by one, the few scientific men who still held out were overborne by the weight of evidence. Geology kept supplying fresh instances of transitional forms; the progress of research in unexplored countries kept adding to our knowledge of existing intermediate species and varieties. During those ten years, Herbert Spencer published his 'First Principles,' his 'Biology,' and the remodelled form of his 'Psychology;' Huxley brought out 'Man's Place in Nature,' the 'Lectures on Comparative Anatomy,' and the 'Introduction to the Classification of Animals;' Wallace produced his 'Malay Archipelago' and his 'Contributions to the Theory of Natural Selection;' and Galton wrote his admirable work on 'Hereditary Genius,' of which his own family is so remarkable an instance. Tyndall and Lewes had long since signified their warm adhesion. At Oxford, Rolleston was bringing up a fresh generation of young biologists in the new faith; at Cambridge, Darwin's old university, a whole school of brilliant and accurate physiologists was beginning to make itself both felt and heard in the world of science. In the domain of anthropology, Tylor was welcoming the assistance of the new ideas, while Lubbock was engaged on his kindred investigations into the Origin of Civilisation and the Primitive Condition of Man. All these diverse lines of thought both showed the wide-spread influence of Darwin's first great work, and led up to the preparation of his second, in which he dealt with the history and development of the human race. And what was thus true of England was equally true of the civilised world, regarded as a whole: everywhere the great evolutionary movement was well in progress; everywhere the impulse sent forth from that quiet Kentish home was permeating and quickening the entire pulse of intelligent humanity.

Why was it that the 'Origin of Species' possessed this extraordinary vitalising and kinetic power, this germinal energy, this contagious force, beyond all other forms of evolutionism previously promulgated? Why did the world, that listened so coldly to Lamarck and Chambers, turn so ready an ear to Charles Darwin and natural selection? Partly, no doubt, because in the fulness of time the moment had come and the prophet had arisen. All great movements are long brewing, and burst out at last (like the Reformation and the French Revolution) with explosive energy. But the cause is largely to be found, also, I believe, in the peculiar nature of the Darwinian solution. True, a thoroughly logical mind, a mind of the very highest order, would have said even before Darwin, 'Creation can have no possible place in the physical series of things at all. How organisms came to be I do not yet exactly see; but I am sure they must have come to be by some merely physical process, if we could only find it out.' And such minds were all actually evolutionary even before Darwin had made the *modus operandi* of evolution intelligible. But most people are not so clear-sighted. They require to have everything proved to them by the strictest collocation of actual instances. They will not believe unless one rise from the dead. There are men who rejected the raw doctrine of special creation on evidence adduced; and there are men who never even for a moment entertained it as conceivable. The former compose the mass of the scientific world, and it was for their conversion that the Darwinian hypothesis was so highly salutary. As Professor Fiske rightly remarks, 'The truth is that before the publication of the "Origin of Species" there was no opinion whatever current respecting the subject that deserved to be called a scientific hypothesis. That the more complex forms of life must have come into existence through some process of development from simpler forms was no doubt the only sensible and rational view to take of the subject; but in a vague and general opinion of this sort there is nothing that is properly scientific. A scientific hypothesis must connect the phenomena with which it deals by alleging a "true cause;" and before 1859 no one had suggested a "true cause" for the origination of new species, although the problem was one over which every philosophical naturalist had puzzled since the beginning of the century. This explains why Mr. Darwin's success was so rapid and complete, and it also explains why he came so near being anticipated.' To put it briefly, *a priori*, creation is from the very first unbelievable; but, as a matter of evidence, Lamarck failed to make evolution comprehensible, or to give a rationale of its mode of action, while Darwin's theory of natural selection succeeded in doing so for those who awaited *a posteriori* proof. Hence Darwin was able to convert the world, where Lamarck had only been able to stir up enquiry among the picked spirits of the scientific and philosophical coterie. Therein lies the true secret of his rapid, his brilliant, and his triumphant progress. He had found out not only *that* it was so, but *how* it was so, too. In Aristotelian phrase, he had discovered the *πῶς* as well as the *ὅτι*.

# CHAPTER VIII.

## THE DESCENT OF MAN.

In 1871, nearly twelve years after the 'Origin of Species,' Darwin published his 'Descent of Man.'

We have seen already that he would fain have avoided the treatment of this difficult and dangerous topic a little longer, so as to let his main theory be fairly judged on its own merits, without the obtrusion of theological or personal feelings into so purely biological a question; but the current was too strong for him, and at last he yielded. On the one hand, the adversaries had drawn for themselves the conclusion of man's purely animal origin, and held it up to ridicule under false forms in the most absurd and odious light. On the other hand, imprudent allies had put forth under the evolutionary ægis their somewhat hypothetical and extravagant speculations on this involved subject, which Darwin was naturally anxious to correct and modify by his own more sober and guarded inferences. The result was the second great finishing work of the complete Darwinian system of things.

Ever since evolutionism had begun to be at all it had been observed that a natural corollary from the doctrine of descent with modification was the belief in man's common ancestry with the anthropoid apes. As early as the middle of the last century, indeed, Lord Monboddo, a whimsical Scotch eccentric, had suggested in his famous book on the origin of language the idea that men were merely developed monkeys. But this crude and unorganised statement of a great truth, being ultimately based upon no distinct physical grounds, deserved scarcely to be classed higher than the childish evolutionism of 'Telliamed' De Maillet, which makes birds descend from flying-fish and men the offspring of the hypothetical tritons. On this point as on most others the earliest definite scientific views are those of Buffon, who ventured to hint with extreme caution the possibility of a common ancestry for man and all other vertebrate animals. Goethe the all-sided had caught a passing glimpse of the same profound conception about the date of the Reign of Terror; and Erasmus Darwin had openly announced it, though without much elaboration, in his precocious and premature 'Zoonomia.' Still more specifically, in a note to the 'Temple of Nature,' the English evolutionist says: 'It has been supposed by some that mankind were formerly quadrupeds.... These philosophers, with Buffon and Helvetius, seem to imagine that mankind arose from one family of monkeys on the banks of the Mediterranean;' and in the third canto of that fantastic poem, he enlarges upon the great part performed by the hand, with its opposable thumb, in the development and progress of the human species. Lamarck, in his 'Philosophie Zoologique,' distinctly lays down the doctrine that man is descended from an ape-like ancestor, which gradually acquired the upright position, not even now wholly natural to the human race, and maintained only by the most constant watchfulness. The orang-outang was then the highest known anthropoid ape; and it was from the orang-outang, therefore, that the fancy of Lyell and other objectors in the pre-Darwinian days continually derived the Lamarckian Adam.

The introduction of the chimpanzee into our European Zoological Gardens gave a fresh type of anthropoid to the crude speculators of the middle decades of the century; and in 1859, Paul du Chaillu, the explorer and hunter of the Gaboon country, brought over to America and Europe the first specimens of the true gorilla ever seen by civilised men. There can be little doubt that the general interest excited by his narrative of his adventures (published in London in 1861) and by the well-known stuffed specimen of the huge African anthropoid ape so long conspicuous in the rooms of the British Museum, and now surviving (somewhat the worse for wear) in the natural history collection at South Kensington, did much to kindle public curiosity as to the nature of our relations with the lower animals. It is no mere accidental circumstance, indeed, that Huxley should have brought out 'Man's Place in Nature' just two years after Du Chaillu's 'Explorations and Adventures in Equatorial Africa' had made the whole world, lay and learned, familiar with the name and features of the most human in outer aspect among the anthropoid family. Thenceforth the gorilla, and not the orang-outang, was popularly hit upon by scoffer and caricaturist as the imaginary type of our primitive ancestors.

On the other hand, during the twelve intervening years immense strides had been made in every department of anthropological science, and the whole tenor of modern speculation had been clearing the ground for the 'Descent of Man,' In 1865, Rolle in Germany had published his work on 'Man Viewed by the Light of the Darwinian Theory.' Two years later, Canestrini in Italy read before the Naturalists' Society of Modena his interesting paper on rudimentary characters as bearing on the origin of the human species. In 1868, Büchner brought out his rudely materialistic sledge-hammer lectures on the Darwinian principle; and in 1869, Barrago flung straight at the head of the Roman clericals his offensive work on man and the anthropoid apes. Most of these foreign publications were unhappily marked by that coarse and almost vituperative opposition to received views which too often disfigures French and German controversial literature. In England, on the contrary, under our milder and gentler ecclesiastical yoke, the contest had been conducted with greater decorum and with far better results. Wallace had broken ground tentatively and reverently in his essay on the 'Origin of Human Races,' where he endeavoured to show that man is the co-descendant with the anthropoid apes of some ancient lower and extinct form. Lubbock's 'Prehistoric Times' (1865) and 'Origin of Civilisation' (1870) helped to clear the way in the opposite direction by demolishing the old belief, firmly upheld by Whately and others, that savages represent a degraded type, and that the civilised state is natural and, so to speak, congenital to man. Tylor's 'Early History of Mankind' (1865) did still more eminent service in the same direction. Colenso's 'Pentateuch and Book of Joshua Critically Examined,' the publication of which began in 1862, had already shaken the foundations of the Mosaic cosmogony, and incidentally discredited the received view of the direct creation of the first human family. McLennan's 'Primitive Marriage' (1865) and Herbert Spencer's articles on the origin of religion had kept speculation alive along other paths, all tending ultimately towards the same conclusion. Darwin's own cousin, Hensleigh Wedgwood, and Canon Farrar, had independently endeavoured to prove that language, instead of being a divine gift, might have arisen in a purely natural manner from instinctive cries and the imitation of external sounds. The Duke of Argyll and Professor Max Müller, by the obvious feebleness of their half-hearted replies, had unconsciously aided in disseminating and enforcing the very views they attempted to combat. Bagehot and Flower, Maudsley and Jevons, Vogt and Lindsay, Galton and Brown-Séquard had each in his way contributed facts and arguments ultimately utilised by the great master architect in building up his consistent and harmonious edifice. Finally, in 1868, Haeckel had published his 'Natural History of Creation,' in which he discussed with surprising and perhaps excessive boldness the various stages in the genealogy of man. These various works, following so close upon Huxley's 'Man's Place in Nature' and Lyell's conclusive 'Antiquity of Man,' left Darwin no choice but to set forth his own reasoned opinions on the subject of the origin and development of the human species.

The evidence of the descent of man from some lower form, collected and marshalled together by Darwin, consists chiefly of minute inferential proofs which hardly admit of deliberate condensation. In his bodily structure man is formed on the same underlying type or model as all the other mammals, bone answering throughout to bone, as, for example, in the fore limb, where homologous parts have been modified in the dog into toes, in the bat into wing-supports, in the seal into flippers, and in man himself into fingers and thumb, while still retaining in every case their essential fundamental likeness of construction. Even the brain of man resembles closely the brain of the higher monkeys; the differences which separate him in this respect from the orang or the gorilla are far slighter than the differences which separate those apes themselves from the inferior monkeys. Indeed, as Huxley conclusively showed, on anatomical grounds alone, man must be classed in the order Primates as only one among the many divergent forms which that order includes within its wide limits.

In his embryonic development man closely resembles the lower animals, the human creature being almost indistinguishable in certain stages from the dog, the bat, the seal, and especially the monkeys. At a very early age he possesses a slight projecting tail; at another, the great toe is shorter than its neighbours, and projects like the thumb at a slight angle; and at a third, the convolutions of the brain reach a point of development about equivalent to that of the adult baboon. In his first stages man himself stands far more closely related to the apes than the apes in turn stand to cats or hyænas.

Rudiments of muscles not normally found in man occur in many aberrant human individuals. Some people possess the power of moving their scalps and wagging their ears like dogs and monkeys; others can twitch the skin of their bodies, as horses do when worried by flies. Mr. Woolner, the sculptor, pointed out to

Darwin a certain little projecting point or knob on the margin of the ear, observed by him in the course of modelling, which comparison shows to be the last folded remnant or rudiment of the once erect and pointed monkey-like ear-tip. The nictitating membrane, or third eyelid, once more, which in birds can be drawn so rapidly across the ball of the eye, and which gives the familiar glazed or murky appearance, is fairly well developed in the ornithorhyncus and the kangaroo, as well as in a few higher mammals, like the walrus; but in man, as in the monkey group, it survives only under the degenerate form of a practically useless rudiment, the semilunar fold. Man differs from the other Primates in his apparently hairless condition; but the hair, though short and downy, still remains on close inspection, and in some races, such as the Ainos of Japan, forms a shaggy coat like an orang's or a gibbon's. A few long rough hairs sometimes project from the short smooth down of the eyebrows; and these peculiar bristles, occasional only in the human species, are habitual in the chimpanzee and in many baboons. Internal organs show similar rudiments, of less enthralling interest, it must be candidly confessed, to the unscientific outside intelligence. Even the bony skeleton contributes its share of confirmatory evidence; for in the lower monkeys and in many other mammals a certain main trunk nerve passes through a special perforation in the shoulder-blade, and this perforation, though now almost obsolete, sometimes recurs in man, in which case the nerve in question invariably passes through it, as in the inferior monkeys. What is still more remarkable is the fact that the perforation occurs far more frequently (in proportion) among the skeletons of very ancient races than among those of our own time. One chief cause why in this and other cases ancient races often present structures resembling those of the lower animals seems to be that they stand nearer in the long line of descent to their remote animal-like progenitors.

The conclusion at which, after fully examining all the evidence, Darwin finally arrives is somewhat as follows:

The early ancestors of man must have been more or less monkey-like animals, belonging to the great anthropoid group, and related to the progenitors of the orang-outang, the chimpanzee, and the gorilla. They must have been once covered with hair, both sexes possessing beards. Their ears were probably pointed and capable of movement, and their bodies were provided with a movable tail. The foot had a great toe somewhat thumb-like in its action, with which they could grasp the branches of trees. They were probably arboreal in their habits, fruit-eaters by choice, and inhabitants of some warm forest-clad land. The males had great canine teeth, with which they fought one another for the possession of the females. At a much earlier period, the internal anatomical peculiarities approached those of the lowest mammals, and the eye was provided with a third eyelid. Peering still further back into the dim abyss of the ages, Darwin vaguely describes the ancestors of humanity as aquatic animals, allied to the mudfish; for our lungs are known to consist of modified swim-bladders, which must once have served our remote progenitors in the office of a float. The gill-clefts on the neck of the human embryo still point to the spot where the branchiæ once, no doubt, existed. Our primordial birthplace appears to have been a shore washed twice a day by the recurrent tides.

The heart then took the shape merely of a simple pulsating vessel; and a long undivided spinal cord usurped the place of the vertebral column. These extremely primitive ancestors of man, thus dimly beheld across the gulf of ages, must have been at least as simply and humbly organised as that very lowest and earliest of existing vertebrates, the worm-like lancelet.

From such a rude and indefinite beginning natural selection, aided by the various concomitant principles, has slowly built up the pedigree of man. Starting from these remote half-invertebrate forms, whose vague shape is still perhaps in part preserved for us by the soft and jelly-like larva of the modern ascidian, we rise by long stages to a group of early fishes, like the lancelet itself. From these the ganoids and then the lung-bearing mudfish must have been gradually developed. From such fish a very small advance would carry us on to the newts and other amphibians. The duck-billed platypus helps us slightly to bridge over the gap between the reptiles and the lower mammals, such as the kangaroo and the wombat, though the connection with the amphibians is still, as when Darwin wrote, highly problematical. From marsupials, such as the kangaroo, we ascend gradually to the insectivorous type represented by the shrews and hedgehogs, and thence once more by very well-marked intermediate stages to the lemurs of Madagascar, a group linked on the one hand to the insectivores, and on the other to the true monkeys. The monkeys, again, 'branched off into two great stems—the New World and Old World monkeys; and from the latter, at a remote period, man, the wonder and glory of the universe, proceeded.'

The word was spoken; the secret was out. The world might well have been excused for treating it scornfully. But as a matter of fact, the storm which followed the 'Descent of Man' was as nothing compared with the torrent of abuse that had pursued the author of the 'Origin of Species.' In twelve years society had grown slowly accustomed to the once startling idea, and it listened now with comparatively languid interest to the final utterance of the great biologist on the question of its own origin and destinies. In 1859 it cried in horror, 'How very shocking!' in 1871, it murmured complacently, 'Is that all? Why, everybody knew that much already!'

Nevertheless, on the moral and social side, the ultimate importance of the 'Descent of Man' upon the world's history can hardly be overrated by a philosophic investigator. Vast as was the revolution effected in biology by the 'Origin of Species,' it was as nothing compared with the still wider, deeper, and more subtly-working revolution inaugurated by the announcement of man's purely animal origin. The main discovery, strange to say, affected a single branch of thought alone; the minor corollary drawn from it to a single species has already affected, and is destined in the future still more profoundedly to affect, every possible sphere of human energy. Not only has it completely reversed our entire conception of history generally, by teaching us that man has slowly risen from a very low and humble beginning, but it has also revolutionised our whole ideas of our own position and our own destiny, it has permeated the sciences of language and of medicine, it has introduced new conceptions of ethics and of religion, and it threatens in the future to produce immense effects upon the theory and practice of education, of politics, and of economic and social science. These wide-reaching and deep-seated results began to be felt from the first moment when the Darwinian principle was definitely promulgated in the 'Origin of Species,' but their final development and general acceptance was immensely accelerated by Darwin's own authoritative statement in the 'Descent of Man.'

To some among us still, as to Lyell before us, this new belief in the animal origin of man seems far less beautiful, noble, and inspiriting than the older faith in his special and separate divine creation. Such thinkers find it somehow more pleasant and comfortable to suppose that man has fallen than that man has risen; the doctrine of the universal degradation of humanity paradoxically appears to them more full of promise and aspiration for the times to come than the doctrine of its universal elevation. To Darwin himself, however, it seemed otherwise. 'Man,' he says, 'may be excused for feeling some pride at having risen, though not through his own exertions, to the very summit of the organic scale; and the fact of his having thus risen, instead of having been aboriginally placed there, may give him hope for a still higher destiny in the distant future.' Surely this is the truer and manlier way of looking at the reversed and improved attitude of man. Surely it is better to climb to the top than to have been placed there—and fallen—at the very outset. Surely it is a nobler view of life that we may yet by our own strenuous exertions raise our race some places higher in the endless and limitless hierarchy of nature than that we are the miserable and hopelessly degenerate descendants of a ruined and degraded angelic progenitor. Surely it is well, while we boast with Glaucus that we indeed are far braver and better than our ancestors, to pray at the same time, in the words of Hector, that our sons may be yet braver and better than ourselves.

# CHAPTER IX.

## THE THEORY OF COURTSHIP.

In the same volumes with the 'Descent of Man' Darwin included his admirable treatise on sexual selection. This form of selection he had already dealt with briefly in the 'Origin of Species;' but as in his opinion it was largely instrumental in producing the minor differences which separate one race of men from another, he found it necessary to enlarge and expand it in connection with his account of the rise and progress of the human species.

Among many animals, and especially in the higher classes of animals, the males and females do not mate together casually; there is a certain amount of selection or of courtship. In some cases, as with deer and antelopes, the males fight with one another for the possession of the females. In other cases, as with the peacock and the humming-birds, the males display their beauty and their skill before the eyes of the assembled females. In the first instance, the victor obtains the mates; in the second instance, the mates themselves select from the group the handsomest and most personally pleasing competitor. Sexual selection, of which these are special cases, depends on the advantage possessed by certain individuals over others of the same sex and species solely in respect to the question of mating. In all such instances, the males have acquired their weapons of offence and defence or their ornamental decorations, not from being better fitted to survive in the struggle for existence, but from having gained an advantage over other males of the same kind, and from having transmitted this advantage to offspring of their own sex alone.

Just as man can improve the breed of his game-cocks by the selection of those birds which are victorious in the cockpit, so the strongest and most vigorous males, or those provided with the best weapons, have prevailed in the state of nature over their feebler and more cowardly competitors. Just as man can give beauty, according to his own standard of taste, to his male poultry, by selecting special birds for their plumage, their port, their wattles, or their hackles, so female birds in a state of nature have by a long-continued choice of the more attractive males added to their beauty and their ornamental adjuncts. In these two ways, Darwin believed, a limited selection has slowly developed weapons like the horns of buffaloes, the antlers of stags, the tusks of boars, and the spurs of game-birds, together with the courage, strength, and pugnacity always associated with such special organs. It has also developed the ornamental plumage of the peacock, the argus pheasant, and the birds of paradise; the song of the lark, the thrush, and the nightingale; the brilliant hues on the face of the mandrill; and the attractive perfume of the musk-deer, the snakes, and the scented butterflies. Wherever one sex possesses any decorative or alluring adjunct not equally shared by the other, Darwin attributed this special gift either to the law of battle, or to the long and slowly exerted selective action of their fastidious mates.

The germ of the doctrine of sexual selection is to be found, like so many other of Charles Darwin's theories, in a prophetic passage of his grandfather's 'Zoonomia.' Stags, the Lichfield physician tells us, are provided with antlers 'for the purpose of combating other stags for the exclusive possession of the females, who are observed, like the ladies in the time of chivalry, to attend the car of the victor. The birds which do not carry food to their young, and do not therefore marry, are armed with spurs for the purpose of fighting for the exclusive possession of the females, as cocks and quails. It is certain that these weapons are not provided for their defence against other adversaries, because the females of these species are without this armour. The final cause of this contest among the males seems to be that the strongest and most active animal should propagate the species, which should thence become improved.'

It must be noticed, however, that Erasmus Darwin here imports into the question the metaphysical and teleological notion of the final cause, implying that the struggle of the males was ordained from without, for this express and preconceived purpose; whereas Charles Darwin, never transcending the world of phenomena, more logically regards the struggle itself as an efficient cause, having for its result the survival of the strongest or the handsomest as the case may be. This distinction is fundamental; it marks the gulf between the essentially teleological spirit of the eighteenth century and the essentially positive spirit of philosophy and science at the present day.

Here again, too, the immense logical superiority of Charles Darwin's rigorous and exhaustive inductive method over the loose suggestiveness of his grandfather Erasmus may easily be observed. For while Erasmus merely throws out a clever and interesting hint as to the supposed method and intention of nature, Charles Darwin proves his thesis, point by point, with almost mathematical exactitude, leaving no objection unmet behind him, but giving statistical and inductive warrant for every step in his cumulative argument. He goes carefully into the numerical proportion of the two sexes in various species; into the relative dates of arrival in any particular country of the males and females of migratory birds; into the question whether any individuals ever remain in the long run unpaired; into the chances of the earliest-mated or most vigorous couples leaving behind more numerous or stronger offspring to represent them in the next generation. He collects from every quarter and from all sources whatever available evidence can be obtained as to the courtship and rivalry of birds and butterflies, of deer and antelopes, of fish and lizards. He shows by numerous examples and quotations how even flies coquet together in their pretty rhythmical aerial dances; how wasps battle eagerly with one another to secure possession of their unconcerned mates; how cicadas strive to win their 'voiceless brides' with stridulating music; how sphinx-moths endeavour to allure their partners with the musky odour of their pencilled wings; and how emperors and orange-tips display their gorgeous spots and bands in the broad sunshine before the admiring and attentive eyes of their observant dames. He traces up the same spirit of rivalry and ostentation to the cock-pheasant strutting about before the attendant hen, and to the meeting-places of the blackcock, where all the males of the district fight with one another and undertake long love-dances in regular tournaments, while the females stand by and watch the chances and changes of the contest with affected indifference. Finally, he points out how similar effects are produced by like causes among the higher animals, especially among our near relations the monkeys; and then he proceeds to apply the principles thus firmly grounded to the particular instance of the human race itself, the primary object of his entire treatise.

Some of the most interesting of the modifications due to this particular form of selective action are to be found amongst the insects and other low types of animal life. The crickets, the locusts, and the grasshoppers, for example, are all famous for their musical powers; but the sounds themselves are produced in the different families by very different and quaintly varied organs. The song of the crickets is evoked by the scraping of minute teeth on the under side of either wing-cover; in the case of the locusts, the left wing, which acts as a bow, overlies the right wing, which serves as a fiddle; while with the grasshoppers, the leg does duty as the musical instrument, and has a row of lancet-shaped elastic knobs along its outer surface, which the insect rubs across the nerves of the wing-covers when it wishes to charm the ears and rouse the affection of its silent mate. In a South African species of the same family, the whole body of the male is fairly converted into a musical instrument, being immensely inflated, hollow, and distended like a pellucid air-bladder in order to act as an efficient sounding-board. Among the beetles, taste seems generally to have specialised itself rather on form than on music or colour, and the males are here usually remarkable for their singular and very complicated horns, often compared in various species to those of stags or rhinoceroses, and entirely absent in the females of most kinds. But it is among the butterflies and moths that insect æstheticism has produced its greatest artistic triumphs; for here the beautiful eye-spots and delicate markings on the expanded wing-membranes are almost certainly due to sexual selection.

The higher animals display like evidence of the same slow selective action. The courtship of the stickleback, who dances 'mad with delight' around the mate he has allured into the nest he prepares for her, has been observed by dozens of observers both before and since in the domestic aquarium. The gem-like colours of the male dragonet, the butterfly wings of certain gurnards, and the decorated tails of some exotic carps all point in the same direction. Our own larger newt is adorned during the breeding season with a serrated crest edged with orange; while in the smaller kind the colours of the body acquire at the same critical period of love-making a vivid brilliancy. The strange horns and luridly coloured throat-pouches of tropical lizards are familiar to all visitors in equatorial climates, and they are confined exclusively to the male sex. Among birds, the superior beauty of the male plumage is known to everybody; and their greatest glory invariably coincides with the special season for the selection of mates. In the spring, as even our poets have told us, the wanton lapwing gets himself another crest. The law of battle produces the spur of the game-birds and the still stranger wing-spurs of certain species of the plover kind. Æsthetic rivalry is answerable rather for vocal music, and for the plumage of the umbrella-bird, the lyre-bird, the humming-birds, and the cock of the rocks. Among mammals, strength rather than beauty seems to have carried the day; horns, and tusks, and spikes, and antlers are here the special guerdon of the victorious males. Yet even mammals show occasional signs of distinctly æsthetic and artistic preferences, as in the gracefully twisted horns of the koodoo, the scent-glands of the musk-deer or of certain antelopes, the brilliant hues of the male mandrill, and the tufts and moustaches of so many monkeys.

It must be frankly conceded that the reception accorded to Darwin's doctrine of sexual selection, even among the biological public, was far less unanimous, enthusiastic, and full than that which had been granted to his more extensive theory of survival of the fittest. Many eminent naturalists declined from the very outset to accept the conclusions thus definitely set before them, and others who at first seemed disposed to bow to the immense weight of Darwin's supreme authority gradually withdrew their grudging assent from the new doctrine, as they found their relapse backed up by others, and refused to believe that the theory of courtship had been fairly proven before the final tribunal of science. Several critics began by objecting that the whole theory was a mere afterthought. Darwin, they said, finding that natural selection did not suffice by itself to explain all the details of structure in man, had invented sexual selection as a supplementary principle to help it over the hard places. Those who wrote and spoke in this thoughtless fashion could have had but a very inadequate idea of Darwin's close experimental methods of enquiry. As a matter of fact, indeed, they were entirely wrong; the doctrine of sexual selection itself, already faintly foreshadowed by Erasmus Darwin in the 'Zoonomia,' had been distinctly developed in the first edition of the 'Origin of Species' with at least as much provisional elaboration as any other equally important factor in the biological drama as set forth in that confessedly introductory work. Nay, Haeckel had caught gladly at the luminous conception there expressed, even before the appearance of the 'Descent of Man,' and had worked it out in his 'Generelle Morphologie,' with great insight, to its legitimate conclusions in many directions. Indeed, the sole reason why so much space was devoted to the subject in Darwin's work on human development was simply because there for the first time an opportunity arose of utilising his vast store of collected information on this single aspect of the evolutionary process. It was no afterthought, but a necessary and inevitable component element of the fully-developed evolutionary concept.

Still, it cannot be denied that naturalists generally did not accept with effusion the new clause in the evolutionary creed. Many of them hesitated; a few acquiesced; the majority more or less openly dissented. But Darwin's belief remained firm as a rock. 'I am glad you defend sexual selection,' he wrote a few years later in a private letter; 'I have no fear about its ultimate fate, though it is now at a discount;' and in the preface to the second edition of the 'Descent of Man,' he remarks acutely, 'I have been struck with the likeness of many of the half-favourable criticisms on sexual selection with those which appeared at first on natural selection; such as that it would explain some few details, but certainly was not applicable to the extent to which I have employed it. My conviction of the power of sexual selection remains unshaken.... When naturalists have become familiar with the idea, it will, as I believe, be much more largely accepted; and it has already been fully and favourably received by several capable judges.'

In spite of the still continued demurrer of not a few among the leading evolutionists, it is probable, I think, that Darwin's prophecy on this matter will yet be justified by the verdict of time. For the opposition to the doctrine of sexual selection proceeds almost invariably, as it seems to me, from those persons who still desire to erect an efficient barrier of one sort or another between the human and animal worlds; while on the contrary the theory in question is almost if not quite universally accepted by just those rigorously evolutionary biologists who are freest from preconceptions or special *a priori* teleological objections of any kind whatever. The half of the doctrine which deals with the law of battle, indeed, can hardly be doubted by any competent naturalist; the other half, which deals with the supposed æsthetic preferences of the females, is, no doubt, distasteful to certain thinkers because it seems to imply the existence in the lower animals of a sense of beauty which many among us are not even now prepared generously to admit. The desire to arrogate to mankind alone all the higher faculties either of sense or intellect has probably much to do with the current disinclination towards the Darwinian idea of sexual selection. Thinkers who allow themselves to be emotionally swayed by such extraneous considerations forget that the beautiful is merely that which pleases; that beauty has no external objective existence; and that the range of taste, both among ourselves and among animals at large, is practically infinite. The greatest blow ever aimed at the Darwinian theory of sexual selection was undoubtedly that dealt out by Mr. Alfred Russel Wallace (et tu, Brute!) in his able and subtle article on the Colours of Animals in 'Macmillan's Magazine,' since reprinted in his delightful work on 'Tropical Nature.' Wallace there urges with his usual acuteness, ingenuity, and skill several fundamental objections to the Darwinian hypothesis of no little importance and weight. But it must always be remembered (with all due respect to the joint discoverer of natural selection) that Mr. Wallace himself, after publishing his own admirable essay on the development of man, drew back aghast in the end from the full consequences of his own admission, and uttered his partial recantation in the singular words, 'Natural selection could only have endowed the savage with a brain a little superior to that of an ape.' It seems probable that in every case an analogous desire to erect a firm barrier between man and brute by positing the faculty for perceiving beauty as a special quasi-divine differentia of the human race has been at the bottom of the still faintly surviving dislike amongst a section of scientific men to sexual selection. Nevertheless, a candid and impartial critic would be compelled frankly to admit that Darwin's admirable theory of courtship has not on the whole proved so generally acceptable to the biological world up to the present time as his greater and far more comprehensive theory of survival of the fittest. It still waits for its final recognition, towards which it is progressing more rapidly and surely every day it lives.

# CHAPTER X.

## VICTORY AND REST.

The last eleven years of Darwin's life were spent in enforcing and developing the principles already reached, and in enjoying the almost unchequered progress of the revolution he had so unconsciously to himself succeeded in inaugurating.

Only one year elapsed between the publication of the 'Descent of Man' and that of its next important successor, the 'Expression of the Emotions.' The occasion of this learned and bulky treatise in itself stands as an immortal proof of the conscientious way in which Darwin went to work to anticipate the slightest and most comparatively impertinent possible objections to his main theories. Sir Charles Bell, in one of the quaintly antiquated Bridgwater treatises—those marvellous monuments of sadly misplaced teleological ingenuity—had maintained that man was endowed with sundry small facial muscles solely for the sake of expressing his emotions. This view was so obviously opposed to the belief in the descent of man from some lower form, 'that,' says Darwin, 'it was necessary for me to consider it;' and so he did, in a lengthy work, where the whole subject is exhaustively treated, and Bell's idea is completely pulverised by the apt allegation of analogous expressions in the animal world. In his old age Darwin grew, in fact, only the more ceaselessly and wonderfully industrious. In 1875, after three years of comparative silence, came the 'Insectivorous Plants,' a work full of minute observation on the habits and manners of the sundew, the butterwort, the Venus's fly-catcher, and the various heterogeneous bog-haunting species known by the common name of pitcher plants. The bare mass and weight of the facts which Darwin had collected for the 'Origin of Species' might well-nigh have stifled the very existence of that marvellous book: it was lucky that the premature publication of Wallace's paper compelled him to hurry on his 'brief abstract,' for if he had waited to select and arrange the whole series of observations that he finally published in his various later justificatory volumes, we might have looked in vain for the great systematic and organising work, which would no doubt have been 'surcharged with its own weight, and strangled with its waste fertility.' But the task that he himself best loved was to watch in minute detail the principles whose secret he had penetrated, and whose reserve he had broken, working themselves out before his very eyes, naked and not ashamed—to catch Actæon-like the undraped form of nature herself in the actual process of her inmost being. He could patiently observe the red and slimy hair-glands of the drosera closing slowly and remorselessly round the insect prey, and sucking from their bodies with sensitive tentacles the protoplasmic juices denied to its leaves by the poor and boggy soil, on which alone its scanty rootlets can properly thrive. He could watch the butterwort curving round the edges of its wan green foliage upon the captured limbs of fly or aphis. He could note how the serried mass of finger-like processes in the utricles of the bladder-wort slowly absorb organic matter from the larva of a gnat, or the minute water-insects entangled within its living and almost animated lobster-pot. He could track the long line of treacherous honey-glands by which the sarracenia entices flies into the festering manure-wells of its sticky pitchers. The minuteness and skill of all his observations on these lesser problems of natural selection inevitably inspired faith among outsiders in the cautious judgment of the observer and experimenter; and day by day throughout his later years the evidence of the popular acceptance of his doctrine, and of the dying away of the general ridicule with which it was first received by the unlearned public, was very gratifying to the great naturalist.

A year later, in 1876, came the 'Effects of Cross and Self Fertilisation in the Vegetable Kingdom.' So far as regarded the world of plants, especially with respect to its higher divisions, this work was of immense theoretical importance; and it also cast a wonderful side-light upon the nature of that strange distinction of sex which occurs both in the vegetable and animal kingdom, and in each is the concomitant—one might almost say the necessary concomitant—of high development and complex organisation. The great result attained by Darwin in his long and toilsome series of experiments on this interesting subject was the splendid proof of the law that cross-fertilisation produces finer and healthier offspring, while continuous self-fertilisation tends in the long run to degradation, degeneration, and final extinction.

Here as elsewhere, however, Darwin's principle does not spring spontaneous, like Athene from the head of Zeus, a goddess full-formed, uncaused, inexplicable: it arises gradually by a slow process of development and modification from the previous investigations of earlier biologists. At the close of the last century, in the terrible year of upheaval 1793, a quiet German botanist, Christian Konrad Sprengel by name, published at Berlin his long unheeded but intensely interesting work on the 'Fertilisation of Flowers.' In the summer of 1789, while all Europe was ablaze with the news that the Bastille had been stormed, and a new era of humanity begun, the calm and peaceful Pomeranian observer was noting in his own garden the curious fact that many flowers are incapable of being fertilised without the assistance of flying insects, which carry pollen from the stamens of one blossom to the sensitive surface or ovary of the next. Hence he concluded that the secretion of honey or nectar in flowers, the contrivances by which it is protected from rain, the bright hues or lines of the corolla, and the sweet perfume distilled by the blossoms, are all so many cunning devices of nature to ensure fertilisation by the insect-visitors. Moreover, Sprengel observed that many flowers are of one sex only, and that in several others the sexes do not mature simultaneously; 'so that,' said he, 'nature seems to intend that no flower shall be fertilised by means of its own pollen.' Indeed, in some instances, as he showed by experiments upon the yellow day lily, plants impregnated from their own stamens cannot be made to set seed at all. 'So near,' says his able successor, Hermann Müller, 'was Sprengel to the distinct recognition of the fact that self-fertilisation leads to worse results than cross-fertilisation, and that all the arrangements which favour insect-visits are of value to the plant itself, simply because the insect-visitors effect cross-fertilisation!' As in most other anticipatory cases, however, it must be here remarked that Sprengel's idea was wholly teleological: he conceived of nature as animated by a direct informing principle, which deliberately aimed at a particular result; whereas Darwin rather came to the conclusion that cross-fertilisation as a matter of fact does actually produce beneficial results, and that therefore those plants which varied most in the direction of arrangements for favouring insect-visits were likely to be exceptionally fortunate in the struggle for existence against competitors otherwise arranged. It is just the usual Darwinian substitution of an efficient for a final cause.

Even before Sprengel, Kölreuter had recognised, in 1761, that self-fertilisation was avoided in nature; and his observations and experiments on intercrossing and on hybridism were largely relied upon by Darwin himself, to whom they suggested at an early period many fruitful lines of original investigation. In 1799, again, Andrew Knight, following up the same line of thought in England as Sprengel in Germany, declared as the result of his close experiments upon the garden pea, that no plant ever fertilises itself for a perpetuity of generations. But Knight's law, not being brought into causal connection with any great fundamental principle of nature, was almost entirely overlooked by the scientific world until the publication of Darwin's 'Origin of Species,' half a century later. The same neglect also overtook Sprengel's immensely interesting and curious work on fertilisation of flowers. The world, in fact, was not yet ready for the separate treatment of functional problems connected with the interrelations of organic beings; so Knight and Sprengel were laid aside unnoticed on the dusty top bookshelves of public libraries, while the dry classificatory and systematic biology of the moment had it ail its own way for the time being on the centre reading-tables. So many separate and independent strands of thought does it ultimately require to make up the grand final generalisation which the outer world attributes in its totality to the one supreme organising intelligence.

But in the 'Origin of Species' itself Darwin reiterated and emphasised Knight's law as a general and all-pervading principle of nature, placing it at the same time on broader and surer biological foundations by affiliating it intimately upon his own great illuminating and unifying doctrine of natural selection. He also soon after rescued from oblivion Sprengel's curious and fairy-like book, showing in full detail in his work on orchids the wonderful contrivances by which flowers seek to attract and to secure the assistance of insects for the impregnation of their embryo seeds. In the 'Variation of Animals and Plants under Domestication,' he further showed that breeding in-and-in diminishes the strength and productiveness of the offspring; while crossing with another stock produces, on the contrary, the best possible physical results in both directions. And now at last, in the 'Effects of Cross and Self fertilisation,' he proved by careful and frequently repeated experiments that a constant infusion of fresh blood (so to speak) is essential to the production of the healthiest offspring. In the words of his own emphatic summing up, 'Nature abhors perpetual self-fertilisation.'

The immediate result of these new statements and this fresh rationale of

Knight's law was to bring down Sprengel forthwith from the top shelf, where he had languished ingloriously for seventy years, and to set a whole school of ardent botanical observers working hard in the lines he had laid down upon the mutual correlations of insects and flowers. A vast literature sprang up at once upon this enchanting and long-neglected subject, the most eminent workers in the rediscovered field being Delpino in Italy, Hildebrand and Hermann Müller in Germany, Axel in Sweden, Lubbock in England, and Fritz Müller in tropical South America. Darwin found the question, in fact, almost taken out of his hands before he had time himself to treat of it; for Hildebrand's chief work was published as early as 1867, while Axel's appeared in 1869, both of them several years earlier than Darwin's own final essay on the subject in the 'Effects of Cross and Self Fertilisation.' No statement, perhaps, could more clearly mark the enormous impetus given to researches in this direction than the fact that D'Arcy Thompson, in his appendix to Müller's splendid work on the 'Fertilisation of Flowers,' has collected a list of no less than eight hundred and fourteen separate works or important papers bearing on that special department of botany, almost all of them subsequent in date to the first publication of the 'Origin of Species.' So widely did the Darwinian wave extend, and so profoundly did it affect every minute point of biological and psychological investigation.

Each of these later works of Darwin's consists, as a rule, of an expansion of some single chapter or paragraph in the 'Origin of Species;' or, to speak more correctly, of an arrangement of the materials collected and the experiments designed for that particular portion of the great projected encyclopædia of evolutionism, of which the 'Origin of Species' itself was but a brief anticipatory summary or rough outline. Thus, the book on Orchids, published in 1862, is already foreshadowed in a part of the chapter on the Difficulties of the Theory of Natural Selection; the 'Movements and Habits of Climbing Plants' (1865) is briefly summarised by anticipation in the long section on Modes of Transition; the 'Variation of Animals and Plants under Domestication' (1868) consists of the vast array of *pièces justificatives* for the first chapter of the 'Origin of Species;' and the germ of the 'Cross and Self Fertilisation' (1876) is to be seen in the passage 'On the Intercrossing of Individuals' in Chapter IV. of the same work. It was well indeed that Darwin began by publishing the shorter and more manageable abstract; the half, as the wise Greek proverb shrewdly remarks, is often more than the whole; and a world that eagerly devoured the first great deliverance of the Darwinian principle, might have stood aghast had it been asked to swallow it piecemeal in such gigantic treatises as those with which its author afterwards sought thrice to vanquish all his foes and thrice to slay the slain.

Yet, with each fresh manifestation of Darwin's inexhaustible resources, on the other hand, the opposition to his principles grew feebler and feebler, and the universality of their acceptance more and more pronounced, till at last, among biologists at least, not to be a Darwinian was equivalent to being hopelessly left behind by the general onward movement of the time. In 1874 Tyndall delivered his famous address at the Belfast meeting of the British Association; and in 1877, from the same presidential chair at Plymouth, Allen Thomson, long reputed a doubtful waverer, enforced his cordial adhesion to the Darwinian principles by his inaugural discourse on 'The Development of the Forms of Animal Life.' A new generation of active workers, trained up from the first in the evolutionary school, like Romanes, Ray Lankester, Thistleton Dyer, Balfour, Sully, and Moggridge, had now risen gradually around the great master; and in every direction he could see the seed he had himself planted being watered and nourished in fresh soil by a hundred ardent and enthusiastic young disciples. Even in France, ever irresponsive to the touch of new ideas of alien origin, Colonel Moulinié's admirable and sympathetic translations were beginning to win over to the evolutionary creed many rising workers; while in Germany, Victor Carus's excellent versions had from the very first brought in the enthusiastic Teutonic biologists with a congenial 'swarmery' to the camp of the Darwinians. Correspondents from every part of the world kept pressing fresh facts and fresh applications upon the founder of the faith; and Darwin saw his own work so fast being taken out of his hands by specialist disciples that he abandoned entirely his original intention of publishing in detail the basis of his first book, and contented himself instead with tracing out minutely some minor portions of his contemplated task as specimens of evolutionary method.

In 1877, in pursuance of this changed purpose, Darwin published his book on 'Forms of Flowers,' in which he dealt closely with the old problem of differently shaped blossoms on plants of the same species. It had long been known, to take a single example, that primroses existed in two forms, the pin-eyed and the thrum-eyed, of which the former has the pin-like summit of the pistil at the top of the tube, and the stamens concealed half way down its throat; while in the latter these relative positions are exactly reversed, the stamens answering in place to the pistil of the alternative form with geometrical accuracy. As early as 1862 Darwin had shown, in the 'Journal of the Linnean Society,' that this curious arrangement owed its development to the greater security which it afforded for cross-fertilisation, because in this way each flower had to be impregnated with the pollen, from a totally distinct blossom, growing on a different individual plant. In a series of successive papers read before the same Society in the years between 1863 and 1868, he had extended a similar course of explanation to the multiform flowers of the flaxes, the loosestrifes, the featherfoil, the auricula, the buckbean, and several other well-known plants. At last, in 1877, he gathered together into one of the now familiar green-covered volumes the whole of his observations on this strange peculiarity, and proved by abundant illustration and experiment that the diversity of form is always due through natural selection to the advantage gained by perfect security of cross-fertilisation, resulting as it invariably does in the production of the finest, strongest, and most successful seedlings. Any variation, however peculiar, which helps to ensure this constant infusion of fresh blood is certain to be favoured in the struggle for life, owing to the superior vitality of the stock it begets. But it is worthy of notice, as showing the extreme minuteness and exhaustiveness of Darwin's method on the small scale, side by side with his extraordinary and unusual power of rising to the very highest and grandest generalisations, that the volume which he devoted to the elucidation of this minor factor in the question of hereditary advantages runs to nearly as many pages as the last edition of the 'Origin of Species' itself. So great was the wealth of observation and experiment which he could lavish upon the solution of a single, small, incidental problem.

Even fuller in minute original research was the work which Darwin published in 1880, on 'The Power of Movement in Plants,' detailing the result of innumerable observations on the seemingly irresponsible yet almost purposive rotations of the growing rootlets and young stems of peas and climbers. Anyone who wishes to see on what a wide foundation of irrefragable fact the great biologist built up the stately fabric of his vast theories cannot do better than turn for instruction to this remarkable volume, which the old naturalist gave to the world some time after passing the allotted span of threescore years and ten.

It was in the same year (1880) that Huxley delivered at the Royal Institution his famous address on the Coming of Age of the 'Origin of Species.' The time was a favourable one for reviewing the silent and almost unobserved progress of a great revolution. Twenty-one years had come and gone since the father of modern scientific evolutionism had launched upon the world his tentative work. In those twenty-one years the thought of humanity had been twisted around as upon some invisible pivot, and a new heaven and a new earth had been presented to the eyes of seers and thinkers. One-and-twenty years before, despite the influence of Hutton and of Lyell, the dominant view of the earth's past history revealed but one vast and lawless succession of hideous catastrophes. Wholesale creations and wholesale extinctions, world-wide cataclysms followed by fresh world-wide births of interwoven faunas and floras—these, said Huxley, were the ordinary machinery of the geological epic brought into fashion by the misapplied genius of the mighty Cuvier. One-and-twenty years after, the opponents themselves had given up the game in its fullest form as lost beyond the hope of possible restitution. Some hesitating thinkers, it is true, while accepting the evolutionary doctrine more or less in its earlier form, like Mivart and Meehan, yet refused their assent on one ground or another to the specific Darwinian doctrine of natural selection. Others, like Wallace, made a special exception with regard to the development of the human species, which they supposed to be due to other causes from those implied in the remainder of the organic scale. Yet on the whole, biological science had fairly carried the day in favour of evolution, in one form or another, and not even the cavillers dared now to suggest that whole systems of creation had been swept away *en bloc*, and remade again in different forms for a succeeding epoch, in accordance with the belief which was almost universal among geologists up to the exact moment of the publication of Darwin's masterpiece.

During the twenty-one years, too, as Huxley likewise pointed out, an immense number of new facts had come to strengthen the hands of the evolutionists at the very point where they had before felt themselves most openly vulnerable. Palæontology had supplied many of those missing links in the organic chain whose absence from the interrupted and imperfect geological record had been loudly alleged against the Darwinian hypothesis in the earlier days of struggle and hesitation. Two years after the publication of the 'Origin of Species,' the discovery of a winged and feathered creature, happily preserved for us in the Solenhofen slates, with lizard-like head and teeth and tail, and bird-like pinions, feet, and breast, had bridged over in part the great gap that yawns between the existing birds and reptiles. A few years later, new fossil reptilian forms, erect on their hind legs like kangaroos, and with very singular peculiarities of bony structure, had helped still further to show the nature of the modifications by which the scale-bearing quadruped type passed slowly into that of the feather-bearing biped. In 1875, again, Professor Marsh's discovery of the toothed birds in the American cretaceous strata completed the illustrative series of transitional forms over what had once been the most remarkable existing break in the continuity of organic development. Similarly, Hofmeister's investigations in the vegetable world brought close together the flowering and flowerless plants, by indicating that the ferns and the horsetails were connected in curious unforeseen ways, through the pill-worts and club-mosses, with the earliest and simplest of forest trees, the firs and the puzzle-monkeys. In minor matters like progress was continually reported on every side. Gaudry found among the fossils of Attica the successive stages by which the ancient and undeveloped civets passed into the more modern and specialised tribe of the hyænas; Marsh traced out in Western America the ancestry of the horse from a five-toed creature no bigger than a fox, through intermediate four-toed and three-toed forms, to the existing single solid-hoofed type with its digits reduced to the minimum of unity; and Filhol unearthed among the phosphorites of Quercy the common progenitor of the most distinct among the recent carnivores, the cats and the dogs, the plantigrade bears and the digitigrade pumas. 'So far as the animal world is concerned,' Professor Huxley said in conclusion, reviewing these additions to the evidence upon that memorable occasion, 'evolution is no longer a speculation but a statement of historical fact.' Of Darwin himself he remarked truly, 'He has lived long enough to outlast detraction and opposition, and to see the stone that the builders rejected become the head-stone of the corner.'

It was in 1881 that Darwin published his last volume, 'The Formation of Vegetable Mould through the Action of Worms.' In this singularly fascinating and interesting monograph he took in hand one of the lowliest and humblest of living forms, the common earthworm, and by an exhaustive study of its habits and manners strove to show how the entire existence of vegetable mould—the ordinary covering of fertile soil upon the face of the earth—is due to the long but unobtrusive action of these little-noticed and ever-active architects. By the acids which they evolve, they appear to aid largely in the disintegration of the stone beneath the surface; by their constant practice of eating fallen leaves, which they drag down with them into their subterranean burrows, they produce the fine castings of soft earth, so familiar to everybody, and thus reinstate the coating of humus above the bare rock as often as it is washed away again in the course of ordinary denudation by the rain and the torrents. It is true that subsequent investigation has shown the possibility of vegetable mould existing under certain conditions without the intervention of worms to any marked extent; but, as a whole, there can be little doubt that over most parts of the world the presence of soil, and therefore of the vegetable growth rooted in it, is entirely due to the unsuspected yet ceaseless activity of these humble creatures.

The germ of the earthworm theory appears to me to have been first suggested to Darwin's mind by a passage in a work where one would little have suspected it—White's 'Natural History of Selborne.' 'Earthworms,' says the idyllic Hampshire naturalist, 'though in appearance a small and despicable link in the chain of nature, yet, if lost, would make a lamentable chasm. For to say nothing of half the birds, and some quadrupeds, which are almost entirely supported by them, worms seem to be the great promoters of vegetation, which would proceed but lamely without them, by boring, perforating, and loosening the soil, and rendering it pervious to rains and the fibres of plants, by drawing straws and stalks of leaves into it; and, most of all, by throwing up such infinite numbers of lumps of earth, called worm-casts, which, being their excrement, is a fine manure for grain and grass. Worms probably provide new soils for hills and slopes where the rain washes the earth away; and they affect slopes, probably, to avoid being flooded. Gardeners and farmers express their detestation of worms; the former, because they render their walks unsightly, and make them much work; and the latter, because, as they think, worms eat their green corn. But these men would find, that the earth without worms would soon become cold, hard-bound, and void of fermentation; and, consequently, sterile.'

If Darwin ever read this interesting passage, which he almost certainly must at some time have done, it would appear that he had overlooked it in later life; for he, who was habitually so candid and careful in the acknowledgment of all his obligations, however great or however small, does not make any mention of it at all in his 'Vegetable Mould,' though he alludes incidentally to some other observations of Gilbert White's on the minor habits and manners of earthworms. But whether Darwin was originally indebted to White or not for the foundation of his theory on the subject of mould, the important point to notice is really this, that what with the observant parson of Selborne was but a casual glimpse, the mere passing suggestion of a fruitful idea, became with Darwin, in his wider fashion, a carefully elaborated and powerfully buttressed theory, supported by long and patient investigation, ample experiment, and vast collections of minute facts. The difference is strikingly characteristic of the strong point of Darwin's genius. While he had all the breadth and universality of the profoundest thinkers, he had also all the marvellous and inexhaustible patience of the most precise and special microscopical student.

For years, indeed, Darwin studied the ways and instincts of the common earthworm with the same close and accurate observation which he gave to every other abstruse subject that engaged in any way his acute intellect. The lawyer's maxim, 'De minimis lex non curat,' he used to say, never truly applies to science. As early as the year 1837 he read a paper, before the Geological Society of London, 'On the Formation of Mould,' in which he developed with some fulness the mother idea of his complete theory on the earthworm question. He there showed that layers of cinders, marl, or ashes, which had been strewn thickly over the surface of meadows, were found a few years after at a depth of some inches beneath the turf, yet still forming in spite of their burial a regular and fairly horizontal stratum. This apparent sinking of the stones, he believed, was due to the quantity of fine earth brought up to the surface by worms in the form of castings. It was objected to his theory at the time that the work supposed to be accomplished by the worms was out of all reasonable proportion to the size and numbers of the alleged actors. Here Darwin's foot was on his native heath; he felt himself immediately on solid ground again. The cumulative importance of separately infinitesimal elements is indeed the very keynote and special peculiarity of the great biologist's method of thinking. He had found out in very truth that many a little makes a mickle, that the infinitely small, infinitely repeated, may become in process of infinite years infinitely important. So he set himself to work, with characteristic contempt of time, to weigh and measure worms and worm-castings.

He began by keeping tame earthworms in flower-pots in his own house, counting the number of worms and burrows in certain measured spaces of pasture or garden, and starting his long and slow experiment in his field at Down already alluded to. He tried issues on their senses, on their instincts, on their emotions, on their intelligence; he watched them darting wildly like rabbits into their holes when alarmed from without, overcoming engineering difficulties in dragging down oddly-shaped or unfamiliar leaves, and protecting the open mouths of their tunnels from intruders with a little defensive military glacis of rounded pebbles. He found that more than 53,000 worms on an average inhabit every acre of garden land, and that a single casting sometimes weighs as much as three ounces avoirdupois. Ten tons of soil per acre pass annually through their bodies, and mould is thrown up by them at an average rate of 22 inches in a century. Careful observations on the stones of Stonehenge; on the tiled floors of buried buildings; on Roman ruins at Silchester and Wroxeter, and on his own meadows and pastures at Down, finally enabled the cautious experimenter to prove conclusively the truth of his thesis, and to present to the world the despised earthworm in a new character, as the friend of man and of agriculture, the producer and maintainer of the vegetable mould on our hills or valleys, and the prime cause of the very existence of that cloak of greensward that clothes our lawns, our fields, and our pleasure-grounds.

It was his last work. Persistent ill-health and equally persistent study for seventy-three years had broken down a constitution never really strong, and consumed from within by the ceaseless fires of its own overpowering and undying energy. On Tuesday, April the 18th, 1882, he was seized at midnight by violent pains, and at four o'clock on Wednesday afternoon he died suddenly in his son's arms, after a very short but painful illness. So retired was the family life at Down that the news of the great biologist's death was not actually known in London itself till two days after he had breathed his last.

The universal regret and grief expressed at the loss in all civilised countries was the best measure of the immense change of front which had slowly come over the whole educated community, in the twenty-three years since the first publication of the 'Origin of Species.' No sooner was Darwin's death announced than all lands and all classes vied with one another in their eagerness to honour the name and memory of the great biologist. Indeed, the spontaneous and immediate nature of the outburst of regret and affectionate regard which followed hard upon the news of Darwin's death, astonished even those who had watched closely the extraordinary revolution the man himself had brought so well to its final consummation. In England, it was felt instinctively on every side that the great naturalist's proper place was in the aisles of Westminster, hard by the tomb of Newton, his immortal predecessor. To this universal and deep-seated feeling Darwin's family regretfully sacrificed their own natural preference for a quiet interment in the graveyard at Down. On the Wednesday morning next after his death, Charles Darwin's remains were borne with unwonted marks, of respect and ceremony, in the assembled presence of all that was noble and good in Britain, to an honoured grave in the precincts of the great Abbey. Wallace and Huxley, Lubbock and Hooker, his nearest peers in the domain of pure science, stood among the bearers who held the pall. Lowell represented the republics of America and of letters. Statesmen, and poets, and philosophers, and theologians mingled with the throng of scientific thinkers who crowded close around the venerated bier. No incident of fitting pomp or dignity was wanting as the organ pealed out in solemn strains the special anthem composed for the occasion, to the appropriate words of the Hebrew poet, 'Happy is the man that findeth wisdom.' Even the narrow Philistine intelligence itself, which still knew Darwin only as the man who thought we were all descended from monkeys, was impressed with the sole standard of greatness open to its feeble and shallow comprehension by the mere solemnity and ceremony of the occasion, and began to enquire with blind wonderment what this thinker had done whom a whole people thus delighted to honour.

Of Darwin's pure and exalted moral nature no Englishman of the present generation can trust himself to speak with becoming moderation. His love of truth, his singleness of heart, his sincerity, his earnestness, his modesty, his candour, his absolute sinking of self and selfishness—these, indeed, are all conspicuous to every reader, on the very face of every word he ever printed. Like his works themselves, they must long outlive him. But his sympathetic kindliness, his ready generosity, the staunchness of his friendship, the width and depth and breadth of his affections, the manner in which 'he bore with those who blamed him unjustly without blaming them in return,' these things can never so well be known to any other generation of men as to the three generations who walked the world with him. Many even of those who did not know him loved him like a father; to many who never saw his face, the hope of winning Charles Darwin's approbation and regard was the highest incentive to thought and action. Towards younger men, especially, his unremitting kindness was always most noteworthy: he spoke and wrote to them, not like one of the masters in Israel, but like a fellow-worker and seeker after truth, interested in their interests, pleased at their successes, sympathetic with their failures, gentle to their mistakes. Not that he ever spared rightful criticism; on the contrary, the love of truth was with him so overpowering and enthralling a motive that he pointed out what seemed to him errors or misconceptions in the work of others with perfect frankness, fully expecting them to be as pleased and delighted at a suggested amendment of their faulty writing as he himself was in his own case. But his praise was as generous as his criticism was frank; and, amid all the toil of his laborious life in his study at Down, he could always find time to read and comment at full length upon whatever fresh contributions to his own subjects the merest tyro might venture to submit for his consideration. He had the sympathetic receptivity of all truly great minds, and when he died, thousands upon thousands who had never beheld his serene features and his fatherly eyes felt they had lost indeed a personal friend.

Greatness is not always joined with gentleness: in Charles Darwin's case, by universal consent of all who knew him, 'an intellect which had no superior' was wedded to 'a character even nobler than the intellect.'

# CHAPTER XI.

## DARWIN'S PLACE IN THE EVOLUTIONARY MOVEMENT.

To most people Darwinism and evolution mean one and the same thing. After what has here been said, however, with regard to the pre-Darwinian evolutionary movement, and the distinction between the doctrines of descent with modification and of natural selection, it need hardly be added that the two are quite separate and separable in thought, even within the limits of the purely restricted biological order. Darwinism is only a part of organic evolution; the theory, as a whole, owes much to Darwin, but it does not owe everything to him alone. There were biological evolutionists before ever he published the 'Origin of Species;' there are biological evolutionists even now who refuse to accept the truth of his great discovery, and who cling firmly to the primitive faith set forth in earlier and cruder shapes by Erasmus Darwin, by Lamarck, or by Robert Chambers.

Much more, then, must Darwinism and the entire theory of organic development to which it belongs be carefully discriminated, as a part or factor, from evolution at large, as a universal and all-embracing cosmical system. That system itself has gradually emerged as a slow growth of the past two centuries, a progressive development of the collective scientific and philosophical mind of humanity, not due in its totality to any one single commanding thinker, but summing itself up at last in our own time more fully in the person and teaching of Mr. Herbert Spencer than of any other solitary mouthpiece. Indeed, intimately as we all now associate the name of Darwin with the word 'evolution,' that term itself (whose vogue is almost entirely due to Mr. Spencer's influence) was one but rarely found upon Darwin's own lips, and but rarely written by his own pen. He speaks rather of development and of natural selection than of evolution: his own concern was more with its special aspect as biological modification than with its general aspect as cosmical unfolding. Let us ask, then, from this wider standpoint of a great and far-reaching mental revolution, what was Charles Darwin's exact niche in the evolutionary movement of the two last centuries?

Evolutionism, as now commonly understood, may be fairly regarded as a mode of envisaging to ourselves the history of the universe, a tendency or frame of mind, a temperament, one might almost say, or habit of thought rather than a definite creed or body of dogmas. The evolutionist looks out upon the cosmos as a continuous process unfolding itself in regular order in obedience to definite natural laws. He sees in it all, not a warring chaos restrained by the constant interference from without of a wise and beneficent external power, but a vast aggregate of original elements, perpetually working out their own fresh redistribution, in accordance with their own inherent energies. He regards the cosmos as an almost infinite collection of material atoms, animated by an almost infinite sum-total of energy, potential or kinetic.

In the very beginning, so far as the mental vision of the astronomer can dimly pierce with hypothetical glance the abyss of ages, the matter which now composes the material universe seems to have existed in a highly diffuse and nebulous condition. The gravitative force, however, with which every atom of the whole vast mass was primarily endowed, caused it gradually to aggregate around certain fixed and definite centres, which became in time the rallying-points or nuclei of future suns. The primitive potential energy of separation in the atoms of the mass was changed into actual energy of motion as they drew closer and closer together about the common centre, and into molecular energy or heat as they clashed with one another in bodily impact around the hardening core. Thus arose stars and suns, composed of fiery atomic clouds in a constant state of progressive concentration, ever gathering-in the hem of their outer robes on the surface of the solid globe within, and ever radiating off their store of associated energy to the impalpable and hypothetical surrounding ether. This, in necessarily brief and shadowy abstract, is the nebular theory of Kant and Laplace, as amended and supplemented by the modern doctrine of the correlation and conservation of energies.

Applied to the solar system, of which our own planet forms a component member, the evolutionary doctrine (in its elder shape) teaches us to envisage that minor group as the final result of a single great diffuse nebula, which once spread its faint and cloud-like mass with inconceivable tenuity, at least as far from its centre, now occupied by the sun's body, as the furthest point in the orbit of Neptune, the outermost of the yet known planets. From this remote and immense periphery it has gradually gathered itself in, growing denser and denser all the time, towards its common core, and has left behind, at irregular intervals, concentric rings or belts of nebulous matter, which, after rupturing at their weakest point, have hardened and concentrated round their own centre of gravity into Jupiter, Saturn, the Earth, or Venus. The main central body of all, retreating ever within as it dropped in its course the raw material of the planetary masses, has formed, at last, the sun, the great ruler and luminary of our system. Much as this primitive evolutionary concept of the development and history of the solar system has been modified and altered of late years by recent researches into the nature of comets and meteors and of the sun's surface, it still remains for all practical purposes of popular exposition the best and simplest mental picture of the general type of astronomical evolution. For the essential point which it impresses upon the mind is the idea of the planets in their several orbits and with their attendant satellites as due, not to external design and special creation, in the exact order in which we now see them, but to the slow and regular working out of preordained physical laws, in accordance with which they have each naturally assumed, by pure force of circumstances, their existing size, and weight, and orbit, and position.

Geology has applied a similar conception to the origin and becoming of the earth's material and external features as we now know them. Accepting from astronomy the notion of our planet's primary condition as a cooling sphere of incandescent matter, it goes on to show how the two great envelopes, atmospheric and oceanic, gaseous and liquid, have gradually formed around its solid core; how the hard crust of the central mass has been wrinkled and corrugated into mountain chain and deep-cut valley, uplifted here into elevated table-land or there depressed into hollow ocean bed; how sediment has slowly gathered on the floor of the sea, and how volcanic energies or lateral pressure have subsequently forced up the resulting deposits into Alpine peaks and massive continents. In this direction, it was Lyell who principally introduced into science the uniformitarian or evolutionary principle, who substituted for the frequent cataclysms and fresh beginnings of the earlier geologists the grand conception of continuous action, producing from comparatively infinitesimal but cumulative causes effects which at last attain by accretion the most colossal proportions.

Here biology next steps in, with its splendid explanation of organic life, as due essentially to the secondary action of radiated solar energy on the outer crust of such a cooling and evolving planet. Falling on the cells of the simplest green plants, the potent sunlight dissociates the carbon from the oxygen in the carbonic acid floating in the atmosphere, and builds it up with the hydrogen of water in the tissues of the organism into starches and other organic products, which differ from the inert substances around them, mainly by the possession of locked-up solar energy. On the energy-yielding food-stuffs thus stored up the animal in turn feeds and battens, reducing what was before potential into actual motion, just as the steam-engine reduces the latent solar energy of coal into visible heat and visible movement in its furnace and its machinery. How the first organism came to exist biology has not yet been able fully to explain for us; but aided by chemical science it has been able to show us in part how some of the simpler organic bodies may have been originally built up, and it does not despair of showing us in the end how the earliest organism may actually have been produced from the prime elements of oxygen, hydrogen, nitrogen, and carbon. Into this most fundamental of biological problems, however, Darwin himself, with his constitutional caution and dread of speculative theorising, was not careful or curious to enter. Even upon the far less abstruse and hypothetical question, whether all life took its prime origin from a single starting-point or from several distinct and separate tribal ancestors, he hardly cared so much as to hazard a passing speculation. With splendid self-restraint he confined his attention almost entirely to the more manageable and practical problem of the origin of species by natural selection, which lay then and there open for solution before him. Taking for granted the existence of the original organism or group of organisms, the fact of reproduction, and the tendency of such reproduction to beget increase in a geometrical ratio, he deduced from these elementary given factors the necessary corollary of survival of the fittest, with all its marvellous and far-reaching implications of adaptation to the environment and specific distinctions. By doing so, he rendered conceivable the mechanism of evolution in the organic world, thus bringing another great aspect of external nature within the range of the developmental as opposed to the miraculous philosophy of the cosmos.

Psychology, once more, in the hands of Herbert Spencer and his followers, not wholly unaided by Darwin himself, has extended the self-same evolutionary treatment to the involved and elusive phenomena of mind, and has shown how from the simplest unorganised elements of feeling, the various mental powers and faculties as we now know them, both on the intellectual and on the emotional side, have been slowly built up in the long and ever-varying interaction between the sentient organism and the natural environment. It has traced the first faint inception of a nervous system as a mere customary channel of communication between part and part; the gradual growth of fibre and ganglion; the vague beginnings of external sense-organ and internal brain; the final perfection of eye and ear, of sight and hearing, of pleasure and pain, of intellect and volition. It has thus done for the subjective or mental half of our complex nature what biology, as conceived by Darwin, has done for the physical or purely organic half; it has traced the origin and development of mind, without a single break, from its first faint and half-unconscious manifestation in the polyp or the jelly-fish to its final grand and varied outcome in the soul of the poet or the intellect of the philosopher.

Finally, sociology has applied the evolutionary method to the origin and rise of human societies, with their languages, customs, arts, and institutions, their governmental organisation and their ecclesiastical polity. Taking from biology the evolving savage, viewed as a developed and highly gifted product of the anthropoid stock, it has shown by what stages and through what causes he has slowly aggregated into tribes and nations; has built up his communal, polygamic, or monogamic family; has learnt the use of fire, of implements, of pottery, of metals; has developed the whole resources of oral speech and significant gesture; has invented writing, pictorial or alphabetic; has grown up to science, to philosophy, to morals, and to religion. The chief honours of this particular line of enquiry, the latest and youngest of all to receive the impact of the evolutionary impulse, belong mainly to Tylor, Lubbock, and Spencer in England, and to Haeckel, De Mortillet, and Wagner on the continent.

In the sublime conception of the external universe and its present workings which we thus owe to the independent efforts of so many great progressive thinkers, and which has here been briefly and inadequately sketched out, Darwin's work in life falls naturally into its own place as the principal contribution to the evolutionary movement in the special biological department of thought. Within the more limited range of that department itself, the evolutionary impulse did not owe its origin to Charles Darwin personally; it took its rise with Erasmus Darwin, Buffon, and Lamarck, and it derived from our great modern English naturalist its final explanation and definitive proof alone. But just as the evolutionary movement in astronomy and cosmical thought is rightly associated in all our minds with the mighty theories of Kant, Laplace, and Herschel; just as the evolutionary movement in geology is rightly associated with the far lesser yet brilliant and effective personality of Lyell; just as the evolutionary movement in the derivative sciences is rightly associated with so many great still living thinkers; so the evolutionary movement in biology in particular rightly sums itself up in the honoured name of Charles Darwin. For what others suspected, he was the first to prove;

where others speculated, he was the first to observe, to experiment, to demonstrate, and to convince.

It should be noted, too, that while to us who come after, the great complex evolutionary movement of the two last centuries justly reveals itself as one and indivisible, a single grand cosmical drama, having many acts and many scenes, but all alike inspired by one informing and pervading unity, yet to those whose half unconscious co-operation slowly built it up by episodes, piecemeal, each act and each scene unrolled itself separately as an end in itself, to be then and there attained and proved, quite apart from the conception of its analytic value as a part in a great harmonious natural poem of the constitution of things. Though evolution appears to us now as a single grand continuous process, a phase of the universe dependent upon a preponderating aggregation of matter and dissipation of energy, yet to Kant and Laplace it was the astronomical aspect alone that proved attractive, to Darwin it was the biological aspect alone, and to many of the modern workers in the minor fields it is the human and sociological aspect that almost monopolises the whole wide mental horizon. No greater proof can be given of the subjective distinctness of parts in what was objectively and fundamentally a single broad psychological revolution of the human mind, than the fact that Lyell himself, who more than any one man had introduced the evolutionary conception into the treatment of geology, should have stood out so long and fought so blindly against the evolutionary conception in the organic world. Indeed, it was not until the various scattered and many-coloured strands of evolutionary thought had been gathered together and woven into one by the vast catholic and synthetic intelligence of Herbert Spencer that the idea of evolution as a whole, as a single continuous cosmical process, began to be apprehended and gradually assimilated by the picked intelligences of the several distinct scientific departments.

Observe also that the evolutionary method has invaded each of the concrete sciences in the exact order of their natural place in the hierarchy of knowledge. It had been applied to astronomy by Kant and Laplace before it was applied to geology by Lyell; it had been applied to geology by Lyell before it was applied to biology by Darwin; it had been applied to biology (in part, at least) by Lamarck and the Darwins before it was applied to psychology by Spencer; and it is only at the very end of all that it has been applied to sociology and the allied branches of thought by a hundred different earnest workers in contemporary Europe. Each stage helped on the next; each was dependent only on those that went naturally before it, and aided in turn the subsequent development of those that naturally came after it.

Nevertheless, the popular instinct which regards Darwinism and evolution as practically synonymous is to a large extent justified by the actual facts of the psychological upheaval. Darwin's work forms on the whole the central keystone of the evolutionary system, and deserves the honour which has been thrust upon it of supporting by its own mass the entire superstructure of the development theory.

For, in the first place, Darwin had to deal with the science of life, the science where the opposition to evolutionism was sure to be strongest, and where the forces and tendencies in favour of obscurantism were sure to gather in fullest force.

Every other great onward step in our knowledge of our own relation to the universe of which we form a part had been compelled indeed to run the gauntlet, in its own time, of ecclesiastical censure and of popular dislike. Those inveterate prejudices of human ignorance which sedulously hide their genuine shape under the guise of dogma masquerading as religion, had long since brought to bear their baneful resources upon the discoveries of Copernicus and the theories of Galileo, as blind, misleading, and diabolical lights, opposed to the sure and certain warranty of Holy Scripture. Newton, again, had in due time been blamed in that he boldly substituted (as his critics declared) the bald and barren formula of gravitation for the personal superintendence of a divine Providence. Laplace had been accused of dethroning the deity from the centre and governance of his celestial system. Around the early geologists the battle of the six days of creation had raged fiercely for nearly half a century. But all these varying modes of thought, though deemed heretical enough in their own day, had touched, as it were, but the minor ramparts and unimportant out-works of the great obscurantist dogmatic strongholds: Darwinism, by openly attacking the inmost problems of life and mind, had brought to bear its powerful artillery upon the very keep and highest tower of the fortress itself. The belief that the various stars, planets, and satellites had or had not been wisely created in their existing positions, and with their present orbits, movements, and relations accurately fore-measured, did not fundamentally affect, for good or evil, the cherished dogmas of the ordinary multitude. But the analogous belief in the distinct and separate creation of plants and animals, and more especially of the human species, was far more closely and intimately bound up with all the current religious conceptions. It was at first supposed, not perhaps without some practical wisdom, that to upset the primitive faith in the separate creation of living beings was to loosen and imperil the very foundations of common morality and revealed religion. The 'argument from design' had been immemorially regarded as the principal buttress of orthodox thought. Theologians had unwisely staked their all upon the teleological dogma, and could ill afford to retire without a blow from that tenaciously defended bastion of their main position. Hence the evolutionary concept had its hardest fight to wage over the biological field; and when that field was once fairly won, it had little more to fear from banded preconceptions and established prejudices in any other portion of the wide territory it claimed for its own.

In the second place, biological evolution, firmly established by Darwin on a safe, certain, and unimpeachable basis, led naturally and almost inevitably to all the other innumerable applications of the evolutionary method, in the domains of psychology, sociology, philology, political thought, and ethical science. Hence the immediate and visible results of its promulgation have been far more striking, noticeable, and evident than those which followed the establishment of the evolutionary conception in the astronomical and geological departments. It was possible to accept cosmical evolution and solar evolution and planetary evolution, without at the same time accepting evolution in the restricted field of life and mind. But it was impossible to accept evolution in biology without at the same time extending its application to psychology, to the social organism, to language, to ethics, to all the thousand and one varied interests of human life and human development. Now, most people are little moved by speculations and hypotheses as to the origin of the milky way or the belt of Orion; they care very slightly for Jupiter's moons or Saturn's rings; they are stolidly incurious as to the development of the earth's crust, or the precise date of the cretaceous epoch; but they understand and begin to be touched the moment you come to the practical questions of man's origin, nature, and history. Darwinism compelled their attention by its immediate connection with their own race; and the proof of this truth is amply shown by the mere fact that out of all the immense variety of Charles Darwin's theories and ideas, the solitary one which alone has succeeded in attaching to itself the public interest and public ridicule is the theory of man's ultimate descent from a monkey-like ancestor. Popular instinct, here as elsewhere profoundly true at core in the midst of all its superficial foolishness, has rightly hit upon the central element in the Darwinian conception which more than any other has caused its fruitful and wonderful expansion through every fertile field of human enquiry.

In short, it was Darwin's task in life to draw down evolution from heaven to earth, and to bring within the scope of its luminous method all that is most interesting to the uninstructed and unsophisticated heart of the natural man.

The application of the evolutionary principle to the world of life, human or animal, thus presents itself as the chief philosophic and scientific achievement of the nineteenth century. Throughout the whole middle decades of the present age, the human mind in all its highest embodiments was eagerly searching, groping, and enquiring after a naturalistic explanation of the origin and progress of organic life. In the vast scheme for the System of Synthetic Philosophy which Herbert Spencer set forth as an anticipatory synopsis of his projected work, the philosopher of development leapt at once from the First Principles of evolution as a whole to the Principles of Biology, Psychology, and Sociology, omitting all reference to the application of evolution to the vast field of inorganic nature; and he did so on the distinctly stated ground that its application to organic nature was then and there more important and interesting. That suggestive expression of belief aptly sums up the general attitude of scientific and philosophic minds at the precise moment of the advent of Darwinism. Kant and Laplace and Lyell had already applied the evolutionary method to suns and systems, to planets and continents; what was needed next was that some deeply learned and universally equipped biological leader should help the lame evolutionism of Lamarck over the organic stile, and leave it free to roam the boundless fields of what Mr. Spencer has sometimes well described as the super-organic sciences. For that office, Darwin at the exact moment presented himself; and his victory and its results rightly entitle him to the popular regard as the founder of all that most men mean when they speak together in everyday conversation of the doctrine of evolution.

On the other hand, the total esoteric philosophic conception of evolution as a cosmical process, one and continuous from nebula to man, from star to soul, from atom to society, we owe rather to the other great prophet of the evolutionary creed, Herbert Spencer, whose name will ever be equally remembered side by side with his mighty peer's, in a place of high collateral glory. It is he who has given us the general definition of evolution as a progress from an indefinite, incoherent homogeneity to a definite coherent heterogeneity, accompanying an integration of matter and dissipation of motion, or, as we should now perhaps more correctly say, of energy. In the establishment of the various lines of thought which merge at last in that magnificent cosmical law, it was Darwin's special task to bring the phenomena of organic life well within the clear ken of known and invariable natural processes.

# CHAPTER XII.

## THE NET RESULT.

And now let us ask ourselves, in all sincerity, what was the final outcome and net result of Darwin's great and useful life?

If Charles Darwin had never existed at all, there would still have been a considerable and expansive evolutionary movement both in biology and in its sister sciences throughout the latter half of the present century. The harvest indeed was ready, and the labourers, though few, were full of vigour. Suppose for a moment that that earnest and single-hearted Darwinian genius had been cut off by some untimely disease of childhood at five years old, all other conditions remaining as they were, we should even so have had in our midst to-day, a small philosophical and influential band of evolutionary workers. Spencer would none the less have given us his 'First Principles' and the major part of his 'Principles of Biology,' with comparatively little alteration or omission. Wallace would none the less have promulgated his inchoate theory of natural selection, and rallied round his primordial conception the very best and deepest minds of the biological fraction. Geology would have enforced the continuity of types; Cope and Marsh would have unearthed for our edification the ancestral forms of the evolving horse and the toothed birds of the Western American deposits. The Solenhofen lithographic slates would still have yielded us the half-reptilian, half-avian Archæopteryx; the tertiary deposits would still have presented us with a long suite of gradually specialised and modified mammalian forms. The Siberian meadows would have sent us that intermediate creature which Prjevalsky recognises as the half-way house between the horses and the donkeys; the rivers of Queensland would have disclosed to our view that strange lung-bearing and gill-breathing barramunda, in which Günther discerns the missing link between the ganoid fishes on the one hand, and the mudfish and salamandroid amphibians on the other. From data such as these, biologists and palæontologists of the calibre of Huxley, Gaudry, Geikie, Rütimeyer, and Busk, would necessarily have derived, by the aid of Wallace's pregnant principle, conclusions not so very far remote from Darwin's own. Heer and Saporta would have drawn somewhat similar inferences from the fossil flora of Switzerland and of Greenland; Hooker and De Candolle would have read pretty much the self-same lessons in the scattered ferns and scanty palm-trees of oceanic islands. Kowalevsky would have seen in the ascidian larva a common prototype of the vertebrate series; the followers of Von Baer would have popularised the embryological conception of the single origin of animal life. The researches of Boucher de Perthes, of Lyell, of Evans, of Boyd Dawkins, of Keller, and of Christy and Lartet, would have unrolled before our eyes, under any circumstances, the strange story of prehistoric man. On the facts so gained, Lubbock and Tylor, Schaafhausen and Büchner, would have built up their various consistent theories of human development and human culture. In short, even without Charles Darwin, the nineteenth century would not have stood still; it would have followed in the wake of Buffon and Diderot, of Lamarck and Laplace, of St. Hilaire and Goethe, of Kant and Herschel, of Hutton and Lyell, of Malthus and of Spencer. The great world never rolls down the abysses of time obedient to the nod of one single overruling Titanic intellect. 'If the doctrine of evolution had not existed,' says Huxley, 'palæontologists must have invented it.'

But Charles Darwin acted, nevertheless, the part of an immense and powerful accelerating energy. The impetus which he gave gained us at least fifty years of progress; it sent us at a bound from Copernicus to Newton; so far as ordinary minds were concerned, indeed, it transcended at a single leap the whole interval from Ptolemy to Herschel. The comparison is far from being a mere rhetorical one. A close analogy really exists between the two cases. Before Copernicus, the earth stood fixed and immovable in the centre of the universe, with obsequious suns, and planets, and satellites dancing attendance in cycle and epicycle around the solid mass, to which by day and night they continually ministered. The great astronomical revolution begun by Copernicus, Galileo, and Kepler, and completed by Newton, Laplace, and Herschel, reduced the earth to its true position as a petty planet, revolving feebly among its bigger brethren round a petty sun, in some lost corner of a vast, majestic, and almost illimitable galaxy. Even so, before Darwin, man stood in his own esteem the fixed point of an anthropocentric universe, divinely born and divinely instructed, with all the beasts of the field, and the fowls of the air, and the fruits of the earth specially created with a definite purpose in subservience to his lordly wants and interests. The great biological revolution, which rightly almost sums itself up in the name of Darwin, reduced man at once to his true position as the last product of kinetic solar energy, working upon the peculiar chemical elements of an evolving planet. It showed that every part of every plant and every animal existed primarily for the sake of that plant or animal alone; it unseated man from his imaginary throne in the centre of the cosmos, teaching him at once a lesson of humility and a lesson of aspiration—pointing out to him how low was the origin from which, in very truth, he first sprang, and suggesting to him, at the same time, how high was the grand and glorious destiny to which by his own strenuous and ardent efforts he might yet perchance some day attain.

That result, inevitable perhaps in the long run, from the slow unfolding of human intelligence, was immensely hastened in our own time by the peculiar idiosyncrasy and lofty personality of Charles Darwin. Without him we should have had, not only evolutionism, but also, as Wallace's discovery testifies, natural selection itself into the bargain. But we should never have had the 'Origin of Species.' We should never have had that vast and enthusiastic consensus of scientific opinion through an all but unanimous thinking world, which has forced an immediate acceptance of evolutionary ideas down the unwilling throats of half unthinking Europe. The prodigious mass of Darwin's facts, the cautious working of Darwin's intellect, the immense weight of Darwin's reputation, the crushing force of Darwin's masterly inductive method, bore down before them all opposition in the inner circle of biologists, and secured the triumph of the evolutionary system even in the very strongholds of ignorance and obscurantism. Without Darwin, a small group of philosophic thinkers would still be striving to impress upon an incredulous and somewhat contemptuous world the central truths of the evolutionary doctrine. The opposition of the elders, long headed even in the society we actually know by a few stern scientific recalcitrants, like Owen and Agassiz, Pictet and Dawson, Virchow and Mivart, would have fought desperately in the last trench for the final figment of the fixity of species. What is now the general creed, more or less loosely held and imperfectly understood, of hundreds and thousands among the intelligent mass, would, under such circumstances, be even yet the mere party-shibboleth of an esoteric few, struggling hard against the bare force of overwhelming numbers to ensure not only recognition but a fair hearing for the first principles of the development theory. It is to Darwin, and to Darwin almost alone, that we owe the present comparatively wide acceptance of the all-embracing doctrine of evolution.

No other man did so much or could have done so much to ensure its triumph. He began early in life to collect and arrange a vast encyclopædia of facts, all finally focussed with supreme skill upon the great principle he so clearly perceived, and so lucidly expounded. He brought to bear upon the question an amount of personal observation, of minute experiment, of world-wide book-knowledge, of universal scientific ability, such as never perhaps was lavished by any other man upon any other department of study. His conspicuous and beautiful love of truth, his unflinching candour, his transparent fearlessness and honesty of purpose, his child-like simplicity, his modesty of demeanour, his charming manner, his affectionate disposition, his kindliness to friends, his courtesy to opponents, his gentleness to harsh and often bitter assailants, kindled in the minds of men of science everywhere throughout the world a contagious enthusiasm, only equalled perhaps among the disciples of Socrates and the great teachers of the revival of learning. His name became a rallying-point for the children of light in every country; and what philosophers and speculators might have taken a century or two more to establish in embryo was firmly grounded, never to be overthrown, by the vast accumulations of fact and argument in the 'Origin of Species,' and its companion volumes.

The end of that great Darwinian revolution the world has not yet seen: in a sense, indeed, it will never see it. For the general acceptance of Darwin's theory, which we may watch progressing around us every minute to-day, implies a complete *bouleversement* of anthropocentric ideas, a total change in our human conception of our own relations to the world and the universe, which must work out for ever increasingly wide-reaching and complex effects in all our dealings with one another and with the environment at large. There is no department of human thought or human action which evolutionism leaves exactly where it stood before the advent of the Darwinian conception. In nothing is this fact more conspicuously seen than in the immediate obsolescence (if one may so speak) of all the statical pre-Darwinian philosophies which ignored development, as soon as ever the new progressive evolutionary theories had fairly burst upon an astonished world. Dogmatic Comte was left forthwith to his little band of devoted adherents; shadowy Hegel was relegated with a bow to the cool shades of the common-rooms of Oxford; Buckle was exploded like an inflated wind-bag; even Mill himself—*magnum et venerabile nomen*—with all his mighty steam-hammer force of logical directness, was felt instinctively to be lacking in full appreciation of the dynamic and kinetic element in universal nature. Spencer and Hartmann, Haeckel and Clifford, had the field to themselves for the establishment of their essentially evolutionary systems. Great thinkers of the elder generation, like Bain and Lyell, felt bound to remodel their earlier conceptions by the light of the new Darwinian hypotheses. Those who failed by congenital constitution to do so, like Carlyle and Carpenter, were, philosophically speaking, left hopelessly behind and utterly extinguished. Those who only half succeeded in thus reading themselves into the new ideas, like Lewes and Max Müller, lost ground immediately before the eager onslaught of their younger competitors. 'The world is to the young,' says the eastern proverb; and in a world peopled throughout in the high places of thought by men almost without exception evolutionists, there was little or no place for the timid group of stranded Girondins, who still stood aloof in sullen antique scientific orthodoxy from what seemed to them the carmagnoles and orgies of a biological Thermidor.

At the same time, it must be steadily remembered that there are many naturalists at the present day, especially among those of the lower order of intelligence, who, while accepting evolutionism in a general way, and therefore always describing themselves as Darwinians, do not believe and often cannot even understand the distinctive Darwinian addition to the evolutionary doctrine—namely, the principle of natural selection. Such hazy and indistinct thinkers as these are still really at the prior stage of Lamarckian evolutionism. It is probable that in the future, while a formal acceptance of Darwinism becomes general, the special theory of natural selection will be thoroughly understood and assimilated only by the more abstract and philosophical minds. Our children will be taught as a matter of course the doctrine of development or of descent with modification; but the rationale of that descent will still remain in all likelihood always beyond the grasp of most of them: just as thousands accept on authority the Copernican astronomy, who would never even be capable of comprehending the simplest proofs of the earth's annual movement round the sun. Thus the name of Darwin will often no doubt be tacked on to what are in reality the principles of Lamarck.

Every day, however, in spite of such half-ignorant adherents, the effects of true Darwinism are widening and deepening. One group of earnest workers is using it now as a guide to physiological, embryological, and anatomical researches. Another is employing it with zeal and skill in the field of classificatory and physiological botany. Yet others are working out its psychological implications, enquiring into instinct and animal intelligence, and solving by its aid abstruse problems of the human mind and the human emotions. One philosopher has brought it to bear on questions of ethics, another on questions of social and political economy. Its principles have been applied in one place to æsthetics, in another place to logic, in a third place to the origin and growth of religion. The study of language has derived new lights from the great central Darwinian luminary. The art of education is beginning to feel the progressive influence of the Darwinian impulse. In fact, there is hardly a single original worker in any department of thought or science who has not been more or less profoundly affected, whether he knows it or whether he knows it not, by the vast spreading and circling wave of the Darwinian conceptions. All our ideas have been revolutionised and evolutionised. The new notions are abroad in the world, quickening with their fresh and vigorous germinal power the dry bones of all the sciences, all the arts, and all the philosophies.

And evolutionism is gradually though slowly filtering downward. It is permeating the daily press of the nations, and gaining for its vocabulary a recognised place in the phraseology of the unlearned vulgar. Such expressions as 'natural selection,' 'survival of the fittest,' 'struggle for existence,' 'adaptation to the environment,' and all the rest of it, are becoming as household words upon the lips of thousands who only know the name of Darwin as a butt for the petty empty jibes of infinitesimal cheap witlings. And Darwinism will trickle down still through a thousand channels, by definite popularisation, and still more by indefinite absorption into the common thought of universal humanity, till it becomes part and parcel of the general inheritance, bred in our bone and burnt into our blood, an heir-loom of our race to all time and in all countries. Great thoughts like his do not readily die: they expand and grow in ten thousand bosoms, till they transform the world at last into their own likeness, and adapt it to the environment they have themselves created by their informing power.

Happy above ordinary human happiness, Charles Darwin lived himself to see the prosperous beginning of this great silent philosophical revolution. Harvey's grand discovery, it has been well said, was scoffed at for nearly a whole generation. Newton's marvellous law of gravitation was coldly received even by the gigantic intellect of Leibnitz himself. Francis Bacon, in disgrace and humiliation, could only commend his name and memory 'to foreign nations and to the next age.' It is too often so with thinkers of the first and highest order: it was not so, happily, with the gentle soul of Charles Darwin. Alone among the prophets and teachers of triumphant creeds, he saw with his own eyes the adoption of the faith he had been the first to promulgate in all its fulness by every fresh and powerful mind of the younger race that grew up around him. The Nestor of evolutionism, he had lived among two successive generations of thinkers, and over the third he ruled as king. With that crowning joy of a great, a noble, and a happy life, let us leave him here alone in his glory.

# INDEX.

## R



## S



## T



## V



## W



## Z

Lector House believes that a society develops through a two-fold approach of continuous learning and adaptation, which is derived from the study of classic literary works spread across the historic timeline of literature records. Therefore, we aim at reviving, repairing and redeveloping all those inaccessible or damaged but historically as well as culturally important literature across subjects so that the future generations may have an opportunity to study and learn from past works to embark upon a journey of creating a better future.

This book is a result of an effort made by Lector House towards making a contribution to the preservation and repair of original ancient works which might hold historical significance to the approach of continuous learning across subjects.

**HAPPY READING & LEARNING!**

LECTOR HOUSE

LECTOR HOUSE LLP

E-MAIL: info@lectorhouse.com

9 789356 146891

9 789356 146891

Printed by Libri Plureos GmbH in Hamburg,
Germany